Japanese
Quality
Circles
and
Productivity

Japanese Quality Circles and Productivity

JOEL E. ROSS
WILLIAM C. ROSS

RESTON PUBLISHING COMPANY, INC.
A Prentice-Hall Company
Reston, Virginia

Library of Congress Cataloging in Publication Data

Ross, Joel E.
    Japanese quality circles and
productivity.

    Includes index.
    1. Quality circles. 2. Industrial
productivity. I. Ross, William (William C.)
II. Title.
HD66.R67   658.4'036   82-3859
ISBN 0-8359-3325-3   AACR2

Copyright © 1982 by RESTON PUBLISHING COMPANY, INC., A Prentice-Hall Company, Reston, Virginia 22090.

10 9 8 7 6 5 4 3 2 1

Printed in the United States of America.

To Carolyn and Carol whose patience and encouragement made this book possible.

Contents

Preface

A paradox exists today in American industry and to a lesser extent in our society. On the one hand, we have become a society of organizations and institutions. Everybody works for one. On the other hand, there is a movement for greater self-fulfillment and job satisfaction, sometimes called quality of work life. Yet, in a classical sense, the "trappings" of the bureaucratic organization are not consistent with these more personal goals. Authority must be enforced, procedures followed, and, above all, control maintained.

This fixation with structure on the part of U.S. managers is unfortunate because it is opposed to personal goals on the job and the people dimension of management. Moreover, we are losing significant productivity and quality that could otherwise be achieved by releasing the potential of the work force. There is a gold mine of potential to be tapped and quality circles offers a way to tap it.

As teachers, practitioners, and students of management, we have witnessed management "movements" come and go. Quality circles is not a movement. It is a way of organizational life. It is not a technique, method, or process. It is a fundamental load-bearing structure that taps the potential of organization members.

This book has two audiences. First, we present the background, logic, and structure of quality circles for those managers who are contemplating using them for both productivity and job satisfaction. Moreover, we provide a framework of actions to be taken. Second, for the "hands-on" facilitator or supervisor, we provide the same background but from a more applied approach. For both audiences, we present an action plan for implementation or self-appraisal if you already have quality circles in place. Throughout we try to balance the two dimensions of productivity and people. As we write this, there is an enormous amount of publicity and press being given to the quality circle phenomenon. We have attempted to sift these sources and provide the reader with the essence of good principles and practice. We have also had access to many companies and individuals who have experienced the use of circles and we summarize this experience. The purpose throughout is to provide a practical guide for those persons who are contemplating quality circles.

Our thanks go to the many supervisors and managers as well as to quality circle members who have found these ideas and methods to be valuable.

Joel E. Ross
William C. Ross

Japanese
Quality
Circles
and
Productivity

1

Why All the Talk About Quality Circles?

QC circles are based on the idea that everyone would like to use his brain in addition to his labor.

JUNJI NOGUCHI, General Manager
Union of Japanese Scientists and Engineers

P utting Japanese management practices "under the microscope" to discover the secrets of Japan's high productivity has become almost an obsession in U.S. business circles. This activity has become so popular that treatises on Japanese methods are crowding other business books off the shelves.

To many business people and public officials in the United States, the postwar success of the Japanese economy is an impressive, yet puzzling, achievement. One may ask: What is it about these strange people who start their working day with a rousing chorus of song about the company, and during the day stop work to have exercise drills? What is it about a company where everybody wears a uniform and refers to others as associates? The overriding question, however, seems to be: Why, when you ask about the success of the Japanese economy, does the name "quality circles" always pop up—why all this talk about quality circles?

For years American business people have hosted armies of Japanese executives visiting the United States in order to learn the latest technology and secrets of American scientific management. Suddenly the tide has turned. United States executives are watching almost helplessly as their customers are snatched away by industrious Japanese competitors selling better products at lower prices. Academics are telling U.S. industry that the most dutiful student of its management practices is now the teacher. American business executives are seeking an idea or two from Japan for themselves. As one wit writes: "It must be hard to get a plane ticket to Tokyo these days. So many American businesses are sending executives there to learn the 'secrets' of Japanese management that reservations must be booked up months in advance."

Just a few years ago the economic power of the United States was unquestioned around the globe. Gradually this has been changing. By almost any measure, the productivity record in the United States can be described only as dismal. Although the American worker remains slightly ahead in absolute output per worker, the gap is closing rapidly as the rest of the world accelerates productivity growth.

The achievements of quality circles in Japan do more than just arouse curiosity when items are reported such as:

- At Nippon Kokan, K. K., the company reports that there are 8,000 workers in 1,480 circles which accounted for more than $86 million in cost savings over a 12-month period through workers' suggestions.
- Nippon Electric Company's Fuchu plant has doubled productivity in three years. Officials estimate that 25% of the improvement is due to worker input.
- In Toyota Motor Company's Quality Circle program 527,718 suggestions were submitted in one year, with 86% of them adopted; about $2.5 million was awarded to workers for suggestions. The company figured a return of five-to-one on the amounts awarded.

When you ask the question, How can 35 Japanese workers produce 350 Datsun car bodies every eight hours, seven times the productivity rate of competing U.S. automakers?, then it is past time to consider the factors that contribute to this success rate.

Not so long ago the label *Made in Japan* was synonymous with shoddy workmanship and poor quality. Yet today, firms like Sony and Toyota sell their products mainly on the basis of quality and high standards. The president of Mitsubishi Heavy Industries, Masao Kanamori, was proud to say: "The existence of our company would be impossible if we failed to reassess our performance in quality, production and cost." This devotion to better value, quality, and innovation at an attractive price has changed consumer preference around the world. Simply, consumers prefer to buy Japanese products.

This change is partly a result of Japan's preoccupation with quality control, a management concept taught by American academics to Japanese industries in the early '50s. From this concept of quality, the process of quality circles emerged. So there is the irony—American executives travel to Japan to learn of a process which originated in the United States.

Quality Circles: Concepts and Characteristics

Myths now exist in the United States that quality circles are unique to the Japanese culture or that they were developed primarily as a participative tool designed for the so-called Japanese style of management. A closer look at the QC process however, reveals that it is based on ideas that have already been expounded for years by behavioral scientists in the United States.

Figure 1-1 defines the term "quality circle" and also identifies its basic concepts. These concepts comprise the premises used to develop the work team. The uniqueness of the QC* idea lies in its emphasis on problem identification and solution. Thus savings and improvement come from a new source, amelioration by workers of problems

---

*We shall use the terms "QCs" (quality circles) and "QC Circles" interchangeably throughout the book. Quality circles are sometimes known as quality control circles (QC circles).

FIGURE 1-1. What Is a Quality Circle?

A quality circle is a small group of employees doing similar or related work who meet regularly to identify, analyze, and solve product-quality and production problems and to improve general operations. The circle is a relatively autonomous unit (ideally about 10 workers), usually led by a supervisor or a senior worker and organized as a work unit. These workers, who have a shared area of responsibility, meet weekly to discuss, analyze, and propose solutions to ongoing problems.

Participants are taught elementary techniques of problem solving, as well as various measurement techniques and quality strategies, including cause-and-effect diagrams, pareto charts, histograms, and various types of graphs.

Some typical efforts in improving methods of production include reducing defects, scrap, rework, and downtime, which are expected to lead to cost reduction as well as increased productivity.

In addition to the above, the circle focuses on the self-development of workers and the improvement of working conditions. Through this process there develops improvement of worker morale and motivation, stimulation of teamwork, and recognition of worker achievements.

Suggested solutions to problems are conveyed by circle members to management through a presentation to management. This includes results of information collection, charts and graphs, and data on estimated quality or productivity improvement. With management's approval, the suggestion is put into operation.

that probably would not have been pursued by supervisory personnel.

VOLUNTARY MEMBERSHIP

An important factor of the quality circle is the spirit of voluntarism. This unique feature, which seems necessary for success, assures the worker that this is not a program "sent down from upstairs by management."

This voluntaristic principle is designed to fit with the expectations of American workers and unions. Should this not be the case, workers will in all likelihood reject the quality circles; past experiences with the "zero defect" and similar movements bring this to mind. If the movement is "mandated" by management, it will suffer from the BOHICA syndrome (bend over, here it comes again!).

TRAINING

Members of the QC are trained in the use of various measurement techniques and quality strategies, including cause-and-effect diagrams, pareto diagrams, histograms and various types of check sheets and graphs (discussed in chapter 9). More advanced circles progress in their training to learn sampling, data collection, data arrangement, stratification, scatter diagrams, and other techniques.

TEAM PROBLEM SOLVING

The process of problem solving contributes to profitability for the firm and also provides an opportunity for worker creativity, thus furnishing a motivational base as well. Through this method of creative problem solving, genuine enthusiasm for innovative suggestions is more likely to emerge.

A GROUP PROCESS

Here the worker learns to work with others cooperatively and becomes a member of the social unit of the circle. The circle provides an opportunity for recognition of the worker's abilities and achievements. Through the leader's efforts, a sense of belonging is accomplished and a spirit of teamwork exists. Circle leaders are instructed in group dynamics so that they may orchestrate the group process better.

A CONTINUOUS PROCESS

The quality circle is not a response to a specific problem; rather it is a continuous study process occurring in the work place. The circle does not wait for some problem to be presented to it but continually looks for problems or ways to improve quality or productivity. It does not stop its activities when a problem has been found and solved.

SUPPORTIVE MANAGEMENT

This means financial support by management for operation costs, implementation of recommendations by the circle, and sponsorship of training seminars. It also implies a willingness by management to devote time and attention to the circle's progress.

RECOGNITION PROVIDED

Firms with quality circles have generally found that participating workers have an enormous craving for recognition. Recognition needs can be met with presentations to management, meetings in the management boardroom, publicity in the plant news, and financial rewards. In this manner, workers can be recognized both financially and otherwise.

MEETINGS ON COMPANY TIME

Circles meet together weekly to discuss, analyze, and propose solutions to quality or production problems. There is nothing sacred about a meeting length of one hour nor a frequency of once a week, but this practice generally represents the best plan. The meetings should be regularly scheduled and not held just when there is some problem. Overtime for after-hours meetings depends upon the company's policy.

Emergence of Quality Circles in Japan

It was surprising how quickly the Japanese work force adopted the idea of quality circles. Why did workers seem so eager to try out a new system?

At the end of World War II, Japan lay prostrate in defeat, her factories bombed, her wartime economy in ruins, and her people discouraged and humiliated. Perhaps the shock of total defeat and the humiliation of being occupied by foreign troops created an atmosphere where there was a willingness to try new ideas. The work force had lost economic and, in many cases, emotional security. They looked to conserve as much as possible of their former lives, but on the other hand they were aware of the need to adapt to the new and changing world around them.

Under these circumstances, it was natural that the Japanese were willing and eager to learn American management techniques. Moreover, they felt that the United States was unquestionably the most advanced industrial nation in the world.

An early postwar effort was organized by U.S. occupation officials to teach wartime industrial standards to Japanese engineers and statisticians. It was thought then that the statistical methods employed in modern quality control activities would be helpful in reconstructing the Japanese industries, almost completely destroyed during the war.

UNION OF JAPANESE SCIENTISTS AND ENGINEERS

One result of this effort to install methods of quality control led to organizing the Union of Japanese Scientists and Engineers (JUSE), a nonprofit association, whose purpose was to provide a standardized collection of information, strategies, and educational programs. JUSE soon became the domestic educational center of statistical quality control and helped develop and promote these ideas and practices for Japanese industry. In addition to disseminating information, JUSE began a massive effort to educate millions of workers and their supervisors in basic quality control methods.

JUSE continues to be the dominant force in promoting Quality Circles throughout Japanese industry. A journal which began publication in 1960 continues to be used today. Entitled *Quality Control for the Foreman*, it includes problem-solving methods to teach supervisors how to improve their abilities and enables QCs all over Japan to learn from each other. In addition to this supervisor's magazine, JUSE offers correspondence courses in quality control methods as well as periodic seminars throughout the country.

INFLUENCE OF DEMING

In 1949 the Union of Japanese Scientists and Engineers sponsored a quality control seminar. In studying the foreign literature that was available at the time, they became familiar with the name and reputation of W. Edwards Deming, a statistician and interpreter of statistics for the federal government. Early in 1950, learning that Deming would be making a visit to advise the post-war Allied occupation government on the use of statistical techniques, JUSE wrote to him asking if he would conduct a seminar for its members. Deming agreed and in July 1950 spoke to an audience composed of the top 50 executives of Japanese industry. Deming recalled: "I told them Japanese quality could be the best in the world, instead of the worst, and they could transform the phrase 'Made in Japan' from a synonym for junk into a hallmark of quality."

Deming's ideas dramatically challenged the JUSE group when he made the prediction that if Japan were to embrace the principles of statistical quality control, the nations of the world would be imposing import quotas against Japanese goods within five years because these goods would be so much in demand. Deming later stated: "They beat my prediction. I had said it would need five years. It took four. They had an uphill struggle against their reputation for bad quality. But within four years they were invading markets the world over and local manufacturers were screaming for protection."

The enthusiasm and the respect for Deming's ideas has been enormous. In 1951 the Union of Japanese Scientists and Engineers established the annual corporate and individual Deming awards. These coveted awards are given to the company that is considered to have achieved the greatest gain in quality. Deming himself is the holder of the Second Order Medal of the Sacred Treasure bestowed on him by Emperor Hirohito for contributions to Japan's economy.

JAPANESE ENGINEERING STANDARDS

The first legislation designed to upgrade the quality of Japanese products was adopted in 1949—the year of the JUSE quality control seminar. This law set up Japanese Engineering Standards (JIS). Under the provisions of this law, companies successful in meeting quality requirements, especially as related to the application of statistical quality control techniques as prescribed by law, were permitted to use this JIS symbol on their products. The Korean War further accelerated the acceptance of these standards. In order to win military procurement orders from the American military between 1954 and 1961, the higher quality standards defined by the U. S. Defense Department had to be met.

JURAN: QUALITY CONTROL AN INTEGRAL PART OF MANAGEMENT FUNCTION

In 1954 Dr. J. M. Juran, noted quality control expert, arrived in Japan for a lecture series. If it can be said that Deming created the enthusiasm for the use of statistical quality control among the leaders of Japanese industry, it can be equally true that Juran introduced a newer orientation to quality control. Juran stated that it must be an integral part of the management function and practiced throughout the firm. In practice, Juran meant teaching quality control to middle management.

To the Japanese, however, the term "middle management" had a different interpretation. In the Japanese reinterpretation, each and every person in the organizational structure from top management to the shop floor worker was to receive exposure to the methods of statistical quality control. Robert E. Cole, Director of the Center for Japanese Studies at the University of Michigan, expressed it best when he wrote, "Workers began to participate in study groups to upgrade quality control practices. This practice gave *both a simple and most profound twist* to the original ideas propagated by the Western experts. Quality control shifted from being the prerogative of a minority of engineers with limited shop experience (outsiders) to being the responsibility of each employee. Each worker, in concert with his or her workmates, is expected to take responsibility for solving quality problems."

The nature of Japanese culture partially explains the willingness of their management personnel to believe in the educability and the potential of even blue-collar workers to contribute to the firm. A comment by Dr. Cole makes this egalitarian approach by Japanese management more understandable: "Japan is a remarkably homogenous country in race, ethnicity, religion, and culture. This means, for all practical purposes, that the Japanese managers can accept the proposition that the average worker is really not so very different from them and that 'there but for the grace of God, go I'." This point may be critical in understanding the willingness of Japanese employers to invest in training blue-collar workers and delegating responsibility to them.

Deming and Juran were not alone in influencing the modernization of Japanese industry. During this period and continuing even today, the Japanese were eagerly seeking information on American management techniques, including all spheres of business and personnel administration. Particular emphasis was given to accumulating information on management theory and practice. The research efforts of the behavioral scientists such as Peter Drucker, Douglas McGregor, Frederick Herzberg, and Abraham Maslow are widely known; and the use of their ideas is a valuable resource to Japanese management. Japanese executives, when visiting American businesses, are often perplexed that U.S. executives seem to know little about the behavioral scientists.

FORMALIZATION OF QUALITY CIRCLES IN JAPAN

Following the impact made by Deming, Juran, Drucker, and other Americans, QC Circles were formalized in 1960 by Dr. Kaoru Ishikawa of Japan. He brought to management's attention the importance of the contributions that these worker groups could make and were making in improving quality and production systems at the local level. Workers were suggesting changes and problem solutions not only in scheduling and in the production process but in design changes of the product as well.

The impetus provided by Dr. Ishikawa caught on rapidly. Exchange visits to other companies, regional and national conventions of quality circles, and visits to plants in America and Europe were among the rewards granted to successful circle members. Today, circles exceed one million with a membership of over six million workers.

Since the initial movement in the early '60s, QCs in Japan have evolved to include several innovations and changes. These include the following:

- Expanding the QC concept to suppliers and subsidiary companies that manufacture parts and provide services to the primary users.

- Expanding activities beyond manufacturing into areas such as maintenance, procurement, administration, and engineering in a variety of white-collar and service firms.
- Forming joint circles across different functions within the company in order to solve intradepartmental problems.
- Holding a variety of conferences, conventions, association meetings, and international visits for the purpose of "cross-fertilization."
- Improving training techniques by including process control charts, advanced statistical methods, regression analysis, and other subjects that go beyond initial problem-solving techniques taught to beginning circle members.

Emergence of Quality Circles in the United States

American manufacturers have looked with increasing interest, if not alarm, at the flow of goods coming out of Japan—goods of better quality that are priced lower than the U.S. product. The capital-intensive United States, home of industrial engineering and the assembly line, production planning and the computer, was witnessing productivity decline in output per working hour while Japan and Western Europe increased their growth rate. The question in the minds of many business people seemed to be: "What has Japan got that we haven't got?"

With that question in mind and with the objective of improving the work atmosphere, the Lockheed Missiles Space Company organized in November 1973 a tour of Japanese industrial plants. The tour group included Wayne Ricker, manufacturing manager, Missiles Systems Division; Donald Dewar, quality control coordinator; William J. Nicol, product assurance assistant manager; Edward P. Rogers, management training coordinator: Louis Bernard, manager, labor relations; and Isamu Yoshioka, manufacturing supervisor and interpreter for the group. This tour began a reversal of the trend in which Japanese study teams traditionally travelled to the United States to observe American business methods.

The Lockheed team was particularly impressed by the workers' involvement in the job. They were also impressed by the level of competence within the circles due in part to the supervisor's leadership. The high degree of training that the workers had received was noted as well. The group agreed that quality circles should not be formed until supervisors were trained and became experienced in solving problems. In addition, the Lockheed team was convinced that to bypass either management indoctrination or supervisors' training would be to jeopardize the success of a quality circle.

In their trip report, the Lockheed group stressed the effectiveness of quality circles in motivating workers by enriching their work experience and increasing their sense of participation. The report also emphasized the strong support given by management to the circle idea. W. S. Riker, one of the visiting Americans, commented: "The highest level management, generally a plant manager, participated in and often led the Circle discussions. Managers demonstrated an amazing [*sic*] detailed knowledge of the Quality Circle program in their respective companies. This convinced me that the programs were not confined to the manufacturing and Product Assurance departments. They were *real, live,* company-wide programs."

After the team members returned from Japan, they recommended installing quality circles in Lockheed. They did this in spite of their reservations about the support needed from management and the time needed for training before the circles could become operative. Despite these reservations, the recommendation was accepted; and the staff decided to begin installing circles on a small pilot scale using the existing organizational structure.

Using training materials translated from JUSE articles the staff developed a training program for leaders, facilitators, and circle members. Each circle was formed with eight to 10 members who did similar work; they would meet once a week for about an hour with the supervisors acting as leaders. The first circle was started in October 1974. By the end of 1975, there were 15 circles, and by 1977 there were 30.

RESULTS OF THE LOCKHEED EXPERIMENT

Following the initial effort in 1974, the results during the next two years were spectacular. With only 15 circles, Lockheed documented savings during this period of $2,844,000. In one operation alone, they had reduced rejects from 25 to 30 per 1,000 hours to less than 6 per 1,000 hours. The ratio of savings to cost of operating was estimated as six to one.

One project illustrates the potential for cost savings. A quality circle in the plastics shop developed a method to mold a plastic part assembly in two steps instead of five. The new assembly was lighter, stronger, and more reliable. Moreover, over the life of the contract, it produced savings of $160,000. Other examples were numerous.

THE QUALITY CIRCLE "TAKE-OFF"

As the news of Lockheed's success appeared in articles and seminars, an increasing number of organizations began to inquire into Lockheed's system. It would seem only natural that many firms in the aerospace industry would be as interested in QC success as Lockheed. Hughes Aircraft, Northrop, Sperry Vickers, and Martin

Marietta were among those firms that started pilot programs.

Westinghouse began experimenting with quality circles in 1978 with seven circles at their Baltimore center. From this start, there are now over 50 company locations where the circles are in effect. At Westinghouse's Baltimore center, Howard Ferguson was in charge of establishing the first quality circle. Speaking of their success, Ferguson concluded: "One prime reason for success is top management's commitment to the program." He also stated that several suggestions by the circles have saved the firm from $50,000 to $100,000. From this beginning, the QC movement has expanded; today hundreds of companies have adapted the technique. *The Wall Street Journal* reported that over half of the companies in the Fortune 500 have implemented or plan to implement quality circles.

The Concept of Quality: United States versus Japan

Because product quality was initially the central focus of QCs in Japan and because many people assume that the major issue considered by a circle is quality, it is important at the outset to place the concept in perspective.

In the United States, the tendency is to check product quality at final inspection in order to separate good products from bad, thus guaranteeing the quality of the outgoing product. If rejects are high or if other problems arise, the quality control department is blamed. There is also the tendency to accept a certain reject rate as a "standard" and thereby vastly underestimate the related costs such as rework, scrap, or customer dissatisfaction.

A fundamental message preached by Dr. W. Edwards Deming is that quality is not something slapped on by inspection of the final product; it must be built in, by operators at every work station in the manufacturing process. Deming stated:

> Quality by inspection is outmoded. A curse of low productivity and loss of market position is total dependence on final inspection. Now of course, no one wishes to produce a defective product, nor to buy it. It is better though, to make it right in the first place, and to know in advance the limits within which the test of the product will fall. Downgrading, re-work, and scrap, are not corrective action. *Corrective action must be built into the process* (italics added).

The Japanese, largely due to Deming's influence, perceive quality and productivity as one and the same. They call it Total Quality Control (TQC). The basic idea is that if you use quality control techniques to raise the level of quality for every corporate activity, you obtain better yields, greater efficiency, higher productivity, and lower costs. The principal features of TQC are the following:

1. All parts of the organization contribute to quality, which has been broadened to include productivity and efficiency. Suppliers are assisted to achieve quality.
2. Top management conducts audits of QC effectiveness.
3. Education and training are required for all personnel from the Board of Directors down.
4. Quality circles are an essential part of TQC.
5. Everyone applies statistical methods. These include statistical tools such as pareto charts, cause-and-effect diagrams, check sheets, scatter diagrams, and control charts.
6. Nationwide QC activities are held to exchange information and ideas.

The Benefits of Quality Circles

To obtain a better grasp of the benefits of circles, we surveyed 24 companies that had significant experience with the process. The company facilitators* were asked to rank the major benefits of quality circles.

In order of frequency of response (priority), their replies were as follows:

Benefit	Ranking (Priority)
Improved Communications	1
Job Satisfaction	2 (tied)
Improved Morale	2 (tied)
Productivity Improvement (other than cost savings)	3 (tied)
Quality Improvement	3 (tied)
Cost Savings	4

It is interesting to note that Improved Communications was in first place by a wide margin.

Additional reasons given by survey respondents include:

1. Development of people.
2. Team building.
3. Respect between workers and management.
4. Development of future leaders.
5. Supervisory growth.
6. Getting commitment to the company.

Based on the above responses, it is clear that the human dimension—the "people" reasons—outweigh

*A facilitator is that individual with primary responsibility for the quality circle effort. He or she organizes and implements the program and coordinates it throughout the company.

cost-savings reasons. This supports both Japanese and American experience and leads to the conclusion that an approach which emphasizes cost savings alone will very likely fail.

The 24 facilitators were also asked whether the overall benefits of circles in their company had been better than expected, about what was expected, or less than expected. Here is the summary of responses:

Response	Number
Better than expected	8
About what was expected	15
Less than expected	1

Do Quality Circles Have a Future in the United States?

Will circles fade as quickly as they came upon the scene? The answer appears to vary with the approach taken by management. Ralph J. Barra, coordinator of the QC program at Westinghouse, stated: "If you emphasize the dollars and cents and make this a management program, it will die out. But if the people embrace it as their program, it can live forever."

Companies with experienced quality circles agree that there should not be too much emphasis on tomorrow's dollar savings or on short-term results. On the other hand, if the emphasis is on a change in management style, the movement will sustain itself and be a viable process. Mr. Barra continued, "Our program is not a cost-reduction program. It is a people-building program that has improved morale and employee-management communication and reduced absenteeism." Dr. J. M. Juran, who began teaching quality control techniques to the Japanese more than 25 years ago said, "Quality Circles can work if companies realize that they're depriving themselves of using the abilities of an educated and creative work-force and use circles as one way to turn that around."

General Motors has about 100 quality circles operating in various plants of its Buick, Chevrolet, Fisher Body, Cadillac, and Oldsmobile Divisions. "This isn't a fad," stated Delmar Landen, GM's director of organizational research and development. "It's part of a fundamental shift toward a new outlook on worker participation in decision making."

Michael Sonduck of Digital Equipment felt that the quality circle will continue being a viable and productive process; however, he issued a caveat regarding its operation. He stated, "If a Quality Circle aims only at improving productivity, it quickly loses worker support. But a program that has only a vague plan of making workers feel better about themselves is likely to collapse for lack of business perspective. Improved job satisfaction and improved productivity go hand in hand, and both are as important to workers as they are to managers."

Much of the future success of quality circles lies in the willingness of American management to profit by the results shown in those circles now operating in the United States. If American management is convinced that hourly rated workers do have an important contribution to make to the organization and are prepared to do so when given the opportunity, then quality circles will have a lasting impact in the United States.

2

The Nature of Quality Circles

American business has treated its employees like children. We've found that they behave differently when they participate.

ALFRED S. WARREN, JR., Vice President
Labor Relations, General Motors

With the accelerating interest in quality circles by American industry, seminars, training institutes, and "how to" manuals for installing this process are proliferating. Many of the concepts used in organization development, group dynamics, and related behavioral approaches will simply be revised to go along with quality circles. This is not all bad. The QC movement is, after all, largely based upon these behavioral concepts. The quality circle process, however, is more than a motivational system designed to make workers "feel good"; it is a system or process involving behavioral science, problem-solving techniques, job-related skills, worker attitudes, and participative management support.

Experience suggests that the QC process, if installed with the proper preparation, including the commitment of top management, can be a valuable tool for increasing productivity, improving quality, and establishing worker job satisfaction. However, in order to achieve these benefits, a proper understanding of the nature of the QC is necessary. The QC should not be viewed as a "quick fix" nor a "package" designed to bring about dramatic bottom-line results. It will not result in overnight improvements in the worker "happiness index." Rather, it is a long-term commitment aimed at significant changes over a period of time. In short, quality circles represent a management philosophy involving an ongoing improvement in organizational climate.

The Quality Circle Philosophy

The QC concept is simple to state but profound in its implications:

> Quality circles are based upon the simple concept that nearly all people will take more pride and interest in their work if they are allowed to make meaningful contributions which influence decisions made about their work.

This philosophy, basic to quality circle success, has been adopted by leading companies using the QC process. One of the first companies to promote QCs was Honeywell, which now has more than 350 active circles. The comment of Jim Widtfeldt, the human resources specialist charged with implementing QCs at Honeywell, reflects the QC philosophy: "Quality Circles must be approached thoughtfully since they are not like short-term programs which can be turned on and off arbitrarily. Quality Circles is a philosophy of management that assumes employees can creatively contribute to solving operational problems if given the chance." Widtfeldt explained further, "They are a form of participative management. You don't jump into something like this without thinking it through. For us, they are a proven method of attacking productivity problems through a process that improves employees' opportunity for achievement, learning, participation and recognition."

Another example is that of Xerox Corporation. President David Kearns, who has established circles throughout that organization, concluded: "Most people are naturally innovative, want to work hard, only don't because management doesn't create the kind of environment where they can. We must prove that we really want to listen if Quality Circles is not to be another passing fad."

Enlightened corporate managers such as Widtfeldt and Kearns are apparently in the minority according to

University of Michigan sociologist Robert Cole, an expert on both Japanese and American labor practices. In his 1979 book *Work, Mobility and Participation,* Cole wrote that in Japan, workers view the corporation as "the sustaining force" of their lives and therefore eagerly cooperate with management. He stated, however, that in the U.S.: "Management writes off worker cooperation because it is seen as either irrelevant or impossible to achieve."

BEHAVIORAL SCIENCE AND QUALITY CIRCLES

The behavioral science basis for circles is certainly no mystery. There has been a plethora of research and publications to support the practice but perhaps as management guru Peter Drucker wrote, "We know nothing about motivation, all we can do is write books about it." Drucker, incidentally, would very likely endorse the Quality Circle movement.

Chapter 5 discusses in more depth the behavioral and motivational principles surrounding the concept of quality circles. At this point, it is useful to summarize these principles as advanced by the noted behavioral scientist Douglas McGregor and suggest how each principle can be *operationalized* by quality circles.

1. The expenditure of physical and mental effort in work is as natural as play or rest.

   Membership in a circle means a participative environment that provides job closure and identification with the work.

2. External control and the threat of punishment are not the only means of getting people to work toward the organization's goals. People will exercise self-direction and self-control toward achieving objectives to which they are committed.

Participation encourages commitment and helps remove the carrot-and-stick management style.

3. Commitment to objectives is a function of the rewards associated with their achievement (esteem and self-actualization, for example).

   The reward in QC membership is more job satisfaction resulting from ownership of the job. Planner and doer are the same thing.

4. Average human beings learn, under proper conditions, not only to accept but to seek responsibility.

   QC membership releases and encourages the natural human desire for increased responsibility — if membership is voluntary.

5. Most people are capable of a relatively high degree of imagination, ingenuity, and creativity in solving organizational problems.

   The primary task of a circle is problem identification and solution.

6. Under the conditions of contemporary industrial life, the average person's intellectual potential is only partially used.

   Experience has demonstrated conclusively that circles release substantial untapped potential.

What Do Quality Circles Consider?

As its name implies, a quality circle devotes a major share of its activity to output quality. However, there are several other interests as well. The distribution of typical circle activities was presented in a study by the American Society for Quality Control (ASQC), published in its book *QC Circles: Applications, Tools, and Theory.* The breakdown of activities was as follows:

Areas of Interest	Percentage of Activity
Quality	22
Efficiency	12
Cost	11
Equipment	10
Morale	10
Process Control	9
Missed Work (Absenteeism)	8
Safety	4
Learning	3
Others	11

Figure 2-1 provides a model or concept of the QC universe. As indicated, the central concerns are (1) quality, (2) cost, (3) specifications, (4) productivity, and (5) schedules. In a manufacturing environment, these concerns are usually impacted by one or more of the "4 Ms": *manpower, material, methods,* or *machines.* As we shall see later, circles identify problems related to the five central concerns and determine problem solutions by a cause-and-effect process that examines the "4 Ms."

QUALITY

The original concept of quality circles as taught by Deming gave emphasis to *statistical quality control* as the answer to improving the quality of Japanese-made goods. As discussed, this concept was changed by Juran and Japanese industry leaders into the concept that quality control was the business of everyone from the blue-collar worker to management. Quality circles now are concerned with the quality of the product, the quality of service, and the quality of working life.

An example of worker concern for quality is vividly illustrated at the Chicago plant of a major electronics manufacturer. When Matsushita Corporation purchased the plant, they installed a Japanese-style system. At the

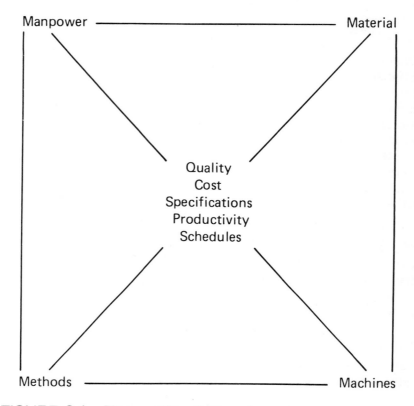

FIGURE 2-1.   The quality circle universe.

time of the purchase, there were 150 defects for every 100 TV sets manufactured. Under Japanese management, the same American work force on the same production line now produces a much higher output of TV sets with only four defects per 100 sets!

COST SAVINGS

There are many examples of cost savings where quality circles have studied problems of the production line and have come up with solutions. At Northrop's aircraft plant in Hawthorne, California, a quality circle of mechanics assembling fighter planes found that expensive drill bits were being broken when boring into the titanium of the aircraft. Through problem-solving analysis, the angle of the drill was changed slightly, resulting in fewer broken bits and a cost savings of $28,000 per year.

SPECIFICATIONS

Not all specifications for a production model are the sole responsibility of the engineers and designers. Quality circle members work toward improvements in cost-cutting and productivity improvement. One example occurred at the solar-turbines division of International Harvester. The assembly-line circle found a way to simplify the production of a compression disc for a turbine. As a result, several production steps were eliminated and $8,700 a year was saved.

PRODUCTIVITY

Quality circles need a lead time when installed, in order to develop a team concept and to begin to define goals. Paul Chaisson of Malden Mills, who heads the quality circle effort, described the beginnings of seven core groups in its retail division: "The groups started meeting last year. The first six months was a purgative period; the workers focused on long-festering complaints about working conditions, apparently testing management's commitment to solve problems. But last fall the groups suddenly began addressing problems involving cost reductions and improved quality." Chaisson commented, "When it gets started, people have an appetite for improving the work that explodes."

The workers made suggestions about the use of materials and tools, and by latest report the percentage of correct fabric inspections had risen within the past year from 88% to 94%.

SCHEDULES

The aerospace industry is notoriously late in meeting schedules and delivery dates (and overrunning costs). Even in the typical manufacturing firm, a 15 to 20% discrepancy between scheduled and actual production is fairly common. Whether this slippage is due to machine downtime, lack of tools or materials, production scheduling or other causes, a QC circle can frequently spot the cause and prevent recurrences.

Additional Objectives of a Quality Circle Program

As mentioned in Chapter 1, among the benefits that company facilitators identify are improved quality, productivity, and cost savings. However, in almost every case these benefits are secondary to the "people" advantages associated with circles. Indeed, most companies that are successful with the circle effort place a higher priority on the industrial relations dimension than they do on bottom-line payoff. In most cases this is a way of saying that the bottom line will take care of itself if we can provide the proper environment to release the workers' potential.

IMPROVE COMMUNICATION

The informal setting of a quality circle opens new avenues in the communicating process. The leader, normally the supervisor, helps to establish an atmosphere within the group where peers can talk to peers about a common interest, thereby facilitating information flow and consensus building. The leader, trained in the skills of motivation, communications, group dynamics, and teaching techniques, is able to develop group cohesiveness and set the stage for group problem solving. The "brainstorming" technique used in problem solving encourages the participation of every member of the circle and develops the communicating skills of each member.

TEAM BUILDING

Behavioral scientists agree that a large part of people's motivation at work is a function of the social environment in which they operate. A circle with a keen sense of identity and a high degree of cohesiveness is much more likely to produce results and be a source of satisfaction and pride to its members. The main benefits of improved identity are the motivational aspects that come from team spirit, the creativity that comes from group participation in problem solving, and the commitment that comes from decisions made through a group process.

Working together through the quality circle process, the group builds the feeling of "team" spirit. Workers may refer to the circle as "my team" or "our team" and, in the spirit of competition with other groups, develop a logo identifying "their circle."

Developing the team-building concept of quality circles is one aspect of the objectives and purpose of the group; it is one of the building blocks inherent in a successfully operating circle.

OPPORTUNITY FOR PROBLEM SOLVING

The heart of the quality circle program is the regular problem-solving meetings in which teams actively identify, analyze, and develop solutions which are within the scope of their responsibilities. They make use of such techniques as data gathering, decision analysis, cause and effect diagrams and management presentations of the solutions. The quality circle is based on the premise that hourly workers are indeed creative, that they are not only able to think, but given the proper environment and tools, they will think and act in a manner constructive to the firm. This process challenges the workers to be more than just the hands that do the work, but instead to actively think and work out solutions that improve the quality of the company's products and increase productivity.

QUALITY IMPROVEMENT AND COST AWARENESS

Many examples abound where quality circles have tackled production-line problems with cost awareness and quality improvement in mind. The most successful groups are those which have accepted the feeling that they are a part of company planning and decision making, instead of the "us versus them" attitude so prevalent in many industries. When a quality circle is able to recognize a problem, come up with the solution, and show management the dollars saved, it fosters the feeling of being a part of the company's total effort.

Before a quality circle is introduced, unnecessary or inefficient operations have often become standard procedure because they have been performed on a routine basis. The circle members begin by identifying the unprofitable functions and determining new methods with cost awareness in mind. It is the team approach of the circles that is the key to the success in improving quality and increasing productivity.

In the Lockheed missiles program, a circle of electronics assemblers producing circuit boards with a high defect rate recommended a solution which resulted in a large dollar cost avoidance and improved quality. Their solution was to spray a protective coating on the boards instead of flow-coating them, a method which trapped air bubbles between layers. The cost avoidance was $19,000 per missile. This is simply another example of the ingenuity and creative ability of the machine operators to come up with solutions to problems.

Problem-solving sessions within a quality circle develop a cost and quality awareness among the workers. For many of the workers, this may be the first time they have ever considered the input cost of labor and materials involved in a production item, or the effects of downtime, rejects, and rework items on the cost and quality of production. Through the process of developing cost-benefit analysis or results measurement, the workers become instilled with a sense of quality and cost awareness.

GETTING PEOPLE MORE INVOLVED

One major advantage of the quality circle process is its positive effect on morale and lessening of dissatisfaction within the work force. Many management experts have advised businesses to concentrate on increasing output per worker at the production-line level through focusing attention on automating assembly lines to turn out more goods with fewer human hands. This approach sets off a wave of spin-off problems such as declining worker morale and rising unemployment in the labor force.

Automation, with its robots, is here to stay; but the human factor will remain on the assembly line. Quality circles are the means of improving worker satisfaction and productivity improvement through getting involved, working toward industry goals, and becoming a part of the decision-making process.

The circle participants in the collective decision-making process identify with the decision and feel committed to its implementation. The behavioral scientists preach that people work harder to implement decisions and strategies that they understand and approve. When the objectives are understood and the group has been trained in problem-solving methods, experience has shown that the implementation is thereby accomplished more intelligently and enthusiastically.

PERSONAL AND PROFESSIONAL GROWTH

Not to be ignored is the higher level of education now existing among the workers from the shop floor up through the levels of management—a work force more capable in their knowledge and ability to contribute to organizational goals. Figure 2-2 illustrates the rise in the level of education among workers from the period of the '60s until the present. With this better-educated work force, the quality circle concept can provide a challenge for personal growth, make use of educational skills, and

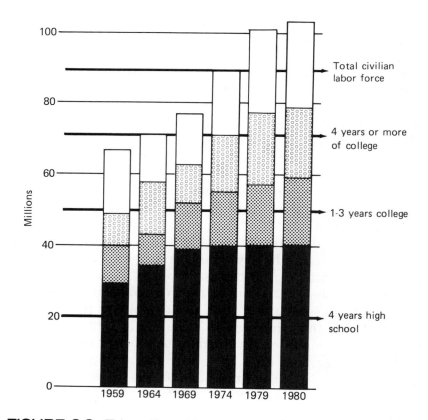

FIGURE 2-2. Educational level of total civilian labor force (*Source:* U.S. Department of Labor, Bureau of Labor Statistics).

provide a means of learning professional skills through the use of quality circle techniques such as pareto analysis, cause-and-effect diagrams, decision analysis, and other problem-solving tools.

Jerome M. Rosow, president of the Work in America Institute, emphasized the changing pattern of the work force when he stated, "We have a different kind of work force today than we've ever had before in this country, and that work force has become more difficult to manage." He added, "The changes in society have been much faster than the changes in the workplace so there's a marked institutional lag between cultural values and work values."

With this growing work force of younger, better-educated, and more demanding workers, there is a lesson here for management in designing the work place. Today's educated work force asks for and demands more than the use of their hands; wages alone do not inform modern workers how important their task is, nor how it ties together with the efforts of fellow workers in a unified whole of worthwhile purpose.

C. Jackson Grayson, Jr., founder of the American Productivity Center, described workers' indifference in these terms: "What has happened is that autocratic, bureaucratic organizations in business and public service have suppressed the desires and ability of the individual to feel that he or she is contributing. People do not mind contributing to the success of an enterprise so long as they feel that they have had a hand in helping to shape it and are rewarded."

Dr. J. M. Juran, president, Juran Enterprises Inc., who began teaching U.S. quality control techniques to the Japanese more than 25 years ago, stated, "If companies realize that they're depriving themselves of using the abilities of a highly educated and creative workforce, the use of Quality Circles is one way to turn this around."

Equally valuable in the quality circle process is the worker's expectation of satisfaction on the job and a sense of personal growth. "I never dared talk to some of these executives before, but here we were telling them how to solve a problem," recalled Janet Burcham, a 24-year-old scheduler in Northrop's facilities department. When Northrop adopted one of her circle's suggestions at an annual saving of about $10,000, she stated, "It really improved my self-image and gave me confidence. Now I feel I can do anything."

What a Quality Circle Is Not

There are those who argue that workers are the same everywhere and that copying the Japanese system of quality control circles will involve only a few adaptations for American managers and workers. Just as the Japanese adapted Western ideas on quality control, so will Americans have to adapt quality control circles to fit the needs of American management and labor. This has been vividly demonstrated in the very use of the term *quality control circles*. Many companies have found that this name itself does not sit well with workers and unions. Specifically, the word "control" has many coercive tones that many firms would prefer to avoid.

The quality circles deal not only with the quality of a product or service but also with the quality of working life. Projects and suggestions deal with safety, improving work methods, worker morale and cost efficiency. In effect, the workers deal with all aspects of the manufacturing operation, and in this sense the groups might better be termed "employee participation circles" or "productivity circles."

THE QC IS NOT A PANACEA

The idea by management that the installation of quality circles will be a "quick-fix" for all of the problems that beset the company can be a hazardous assumption. Management may seize upon quality circles as the one and only cure for motivation, productivity, and quality problems. Installing quality circles does not preclude continuing efforts through avenues already established within the company.

Experience has shown that the quality circle is not the "cure-all" for every phase of work within the company. There are many items that are considered outside the circle's responsibilities. These generally include the following:

1. Benefits and salaries
2. Grievances
3. Hiring and firing practices of the company.

There are normal channels for these matters, and they are not the responsibility of the circle.

A QC IS NOT A SURE SUCCESS

There is the danger that the glowing reports about the success of quality circles may be an "oversell" to managers considering starting up this process in the company. Little attention has been given to the failures, mostly undocumented, and still less to those quality circles that limp along, accomplishing little.

Installing quality circles as a program is a long and careful process with too few persons around with the experience and expertise necessary to establish a viable program in the company.

In the quality circle "chain" (i.e., management, the steering committee, the facilitator, the coordinator, the leader, and circle members), the success depends upon the interaction of the whole. The old expression of the "weakest link" is appropriate here in that it can stop the flow of support and interaction necessary for the endeavor's success.

It can be quickly determined from the above that the installation of quality circles is no quick-and-easy solution that will increase productivity and lead to success. Instead, this carefully designed process requires the motivation and cooperation of management, the union (if applicable), and labor. It is a basic managerial philosophy that requires time and effort to be established as a cooperative effort throughout the organization.

A QC IS NOT A MANAGEMENT PLOY TO USE EMPLOYEES

Past practices of management, such as an autocratic (theory X) and "top-down" approach, may cause the workers to be suspicious that the QC is just another program that is being forced upon them. If the wrong attitude exists in management personnel, the labor force will lack interest in adopting the program.

Management people must not "use" circles to further their own pet ideas or projects. Rather, circles must be free to choose their own priorities. Careful thought has to be given to the union's position. If a union perceives that management is using circles as another attempt to squeeze more productivity from members without sharing rewards, or if it fears that the system will create a wedge between the workers and the union, it will be difficult to get the program off the ground.

A QC IS NOT A FORUM FOR GRIEVANCES

The circle's activity focuses on working on problems of quality, productivity, and cost-cutting. Becoming involved in working conditions, pay rates, employment practices, and "personalities" interferes with the circle's objectives. Here again, many of these subjects are proper concerns of the union and management and should be addressed as such. Whether there is a union or not, there are proper channels, other than the circle, for grievances.

A QC IS NOT AN INNOVATION THAT MANAGERS SHOULD FEAR

Many supervisors, up to and including middle management, will be at best indifferent and often may be hostile to quality circles, which challenge existing and familiar adversary relationships. If middle-level personnel are bypassed when the new program is being established, they understandably fail to develop a strong commitment to it. Instead, they see it as a threat to their power and status.

Simply installing quality circles in an organization without proper preparation is a sure guarantee of failure. The circle alone, without proper support, without proper training, and without the right leadership, is already on rocky ground with little chance to be effective.

Special management skills and philosophies must be in the making or in place before quality circles can be installed with success. The organization must be convinced that the key to productivity lies in its workers, and that these workers' commitment, involvement, and participation, with some degree of self-management, are the keys to making the circle a successful entity within the company.

ACCENTUATE THE POSITIVE

Listing the descriptions of "What a Quality Circle Is Not" appears on the surface to have a negative connotation for circles. On the contrary, however, the purpose is to give warning signals for avoiding some of the traps that can be encountered unless the approach to quality circles is well thought out and proper planning precedes the installation of the process. The admonition might be, "Go slow. Think it through."

The quality circle concept is a major change in the thinking of managers and production-line supervisors. This philosophy may require new attitudes. A program which is carefully prepared and slowly implemented will be less threatening to workers, unions, supervisors, and middle management.

3

Productivity in the United States

When productivity slows you have fewer goods, fewer jobs, more social tensions, more inflation, reduced profits and a lower standard of living.

C. JACKSON GRAYSON, JR., Chairman
American Productivity Center

In discussing the topic of productivity with a group of U.S. Chamber of Commerce executives, Commerce Secretary Malcolm Baldridge remarked, "I don't think labor productivity is the problem, it's management, and I speak as a former manager. In my opinion, management has been too fat, dumb and happy in the past ten years."

This statement was made for the purpose of gaining support for the Reagan administration's economic program, otherwise known as Reaganomics or "supply-side economics." The primary objective of this program is to improve the productivity of American industry by encouraging greater investment in our capital stock.

The concern over productivity is a fairly recent development. Several years ago, Richard Gerstenberg, former chairman of General Motors, said he was astonished at how few major companies "even know what productivity is." In the mid-1970s a survey of 6,000 business managers, conducted by the American Management Association, found serious worry over productivity, but two thirds of the respondents in the survey reported that their companies were making no special effort to evaluate the problem. At that time, it was estimated that fewer than 100 major corporations have in place a comprehensive productivity improvement program. Fortunately the concern is growing, and today productivity is on everyone's mind. Quality circles can help.

Many managers will endorse productivity as a good thing but when pressed to describe what they are doing about it will say, "Yes, we have a cost reduction drive . . . or an MBO program . . . a suggestion box . . . cash awards . . . an incentive program," and so on. These techniques are all right but do not comprise a planned program. Indeed, few managers can really define, measure, plan for, or even understand the topic. Too often any effort in this direction has a short-run financial improvement as its objective rather than long-run, systematic, or comprehensive programs.

What then, is happening to American productivity? Will the United States become, as economist Arthur Laffer suggests, the fastest "underdeveloping" country in the world?

Decline of Productivity

By almost any measure, the productivity record in the United States can only be described as dismal. Although the American worker remains slightly ahead in absolute output per worker, the gap is closing rapidly as the rest of the industrial world accelerates productivity growth. The plight of the domestic steel industry needs little explanation. This industry has been plagued for years by stagnating productivity and soaring operating costs. In the automobile industry the Japanese can make a car and ship it here for $1,500 less than it costs GM or Ford to produce and sell a comparable vehicle.

The capital-intensive United States—home of industrial engineering and the assembly line, production planning and the computer—has recently witnessed the first significant productivity decline in three decades in output per working hour. Japan and the leading nations of Western Europe bettered us in rate of growth as we fell to seventh place—last place among the industrial nations of the world (see Table 3-1). In the 1980's, relative lack of growth has become a critical issue for the United States.

Reversing this trend is of substantial concern to each of us. At the *national* level, this is the best way to stop inflation and improve real income. At the *company* level, this is the only way to reduce costs and improve

TABLE 3-1
Manufacturing Productivity
(Major Industrial Economies, 1960—1980,
Average Annual Rates of Change)

Country	Productivity Growth
Japan	9.3
Netherlands	7.4
Belgium	7.3
Denmark	6.6
Italy	5.9
France	5.5
Germany	5.4
Sweden	5.4
Canada	3.8
United Kingdom	3.2
United States	2.7

Source: U.S. Department of Labor, Bureau of Labor Statistics.

profits. Increased productivity allows organizations to give customers more product value per dollar; compete more effectively in the market place; use resources more effectively; and increase sales volume, profits, and return on investment.

Consequences of the Decline

The reaction to the decline in American productivity is typified by this comment from the president of Chase Manhattan Bank: "My fear is that if this trend continues, our standard of living will steadily sink and our nation will become a second-rate industrial power before this century ends." Although the productivity decline pervades all aspects of our lives, the three aspects of most concern are the national economy, the standard of living, and the continuing inflation.

The impact on the *national economy* was summarized by the Joint Economic Committee of the U.S. Congress when it concluded: "Productivity is the economic linchpin of the 1980s." Productivity is the "holding together" of the economy. Aside from the internal consequence of the problem, our external situation is adversely affected as evidenced by the declining trade balance. This deterioration can be traced directly to our reduced relative standing among industrialized nations with respect to productivity growth.

The impact on our *standard of living* is both personal and dramatic. The average American household is now earning about $4000 *less* than what it would have earned had our nation maintained its 3% productivity growth of the 1950s and 1960s. We now have a real income gap—the difference between what we are earning and what we could earn. In 1980 Federal Reserve Chairman Paul Volcker summarized the problem as follows: "When productivity is declining, there isn't any way you can increase your standard of living in the nation as a whole just by asking for higher wages or prices."

Double-digit *inflation*, accompanied by the debilitating fall of the dollar, can be traced directly to the slow growth in productivity. This *decline* in the rate of growth, accompanied by *increases* in wages and compensation, gives us the "productivity gap," a reliable measure of inflation pressures. Table 3-2 shows the dramatic decline of the rate of productivity growth for selected periods in the United States. When the figures in this table are matched with wage increases for the same period, we get the approximate inflation rate. While this is not the whole story of inflation, it is a significant part of the story.

Why Has Productivity Declined?

When it comes to naming causes for this "productivity crisis," every economist, industrialist, and governmental

TABLE 3-2
Annual Manufacturing Productivity
Growth in the United States
(Output per Manhour)

Period	Average Annual Rate of Change
1960-1970	2.9
1970-1980	2.4
1973-1980	1.7
1977-1978	0.9
1978-1979	1.0
1979-1980	−0.5

Source: U.S. Department of Labor, Bureau of Labor Statistics.

official seems to have a favorite culprit. Among the most popular explanations are that the problem springs from:

1. A labor force increasingly affected by poor motivation, declining skills, and union-fed uncooperative attitudes.
2. Government tying industry's hands with over-taxation and overregulation while bailing out antiquated industries at the expense of fresh growth.
3. Inflation drying up investment capital, depriving industry of the money urgently needed for new plants, modern equipment, and research and development.
4. Escalating energy costs.

Workers have been natural prime targets for criticism, since they mark the spot where productivity is measured. In a survey recently conducted by *Productivity*, a monthly newsletter, American managers were asked to rank several factors as obstacles to productivity. The survey generated 221 responses from managers and executives representing a wide variety of companies and organizations. The overwhelming majority chose "poor management" as the greatest obstacle. Government regulations took second place in the rankings, followed closely by insufficient capital spending, inadequate training of the work force, and insufficient investment in research and development. Contrary to much of what is heard today, a declining work ethic as a hurdle to productivity growth was placed at the bottom of the list.

On any given day, the business press will contain dozens of references to the causes and cures of the productivity decline. The general public has heard so frequently that productivity growth is the main cause of the country's relative economic decline that it has started to take the subject seriously.

Interest and pressure groups continue to suggest remedies that are self-serving and promise to do most to feather their own nests. Wall Street argues for the elimination of "phantom" capital gains and the "double tax" on dividends, contending that this cure will provide more risk capital to the industry. Corporations lobby for relaxed government regulations so that more funds can be diverted to capital investment and plant improvement. Unions maintain that corporations export work to foreign countries with low labor rates rather than modernize the U.S. plant. And so it goes—everyone has a pet reason.

Economists and others get pretty abstruse over just exactly what is meant by productivity and the real reasons for its decline; still, certain hard facts are plain enough. The U.S. lead in high-technology exports is being rapidly nibbled away; foreign imports to this country are increasing; and some significant foreign industries are showing stronger productivity gains than are being registered in comparable U.S. industries.

Despite the debate over the several causes that are advanced for the productivity decline, the underlying reasons are still somewhat puzzling. The answer seems to lie in a number of influences that combine to explain the pattern of retardation. Some of these are examined below.

MANAGEMENT'S INATTENTION

U.S. Secretary of Commerce Malcolm Baldridge, speaking in Chicago recently, stated: "Between our own complacency and the rise of management expertise around the world, we now too often do a second-rate job of management, compared to our foreign competitors." Echoing this thought, Bell & Howell Company Chairman Donald Frey's bad news for business managers is that their own poor performance is largely responsible for productivity problems. Specifically, Frey said, American management must develop products and improve purchasing, planning, and scheduling to cut down on material costs, which average 57% of sales revenues for manufacturers.

A recent study of successful corporations by the management consultants, A. T. Kearney, Inc., agreed that the key to productivity is better management—not continued attempts to produce more pounds of automobile per worker.

Management personnel in many companies often limit their view of productivity improvement to the replacement of labor with capital equipment. But labor is only one determinant of productivity. The broader definition of productivity favored by the American Productivity Center includes all the elements of labor, capital, energy, and materials that go into producing goods and services. This broader perspective diminishes the focus on short-term gains through employee reduction and enhances awareness of a number of techniques which have important long-run productivity impact.

Productivity is somewhat like the weather; many managers are talking about it, but few are doing anything. If you ask the question, Who's in charge of productivity?, the typical answer in most firms would be, "Nobody!"

Some industries are particularly lax in efficiency. This laxity appears to be higher than average in service industries which make up about 50% of our gross national product. When you combine this with the "service" or overhead departments of other types of business, you have an enormous sector that is not being gauged by any value-added measure. A senior executive in a large insurance company said, "The service industries cannot answer some of the basic questions relating to their operation. We spent three years installing our information system but we can't tell how much it cost since we don't have a cost accounting system to tell us. However, as slow as the insurance industry is, it appears that the banking industry is still behind us."

The public sector—*government*—is the largest industry in the United States and leads the downhill productivity race. Since 1961 the U.S. population has risen by 23%, but government employees have climbed from 34% in the U.S. Department of Agriculture to 157% in the federal court system.

GOVERNMENT REGULATIONS

There is no question but that government regulations are responsible for slower productivity growth. Although no accurate measures are available, some estimates suggest that the cost in lost productivity could add up to as much as 2% of the gross national product. And how can you put a value on the diversion of executive attention from matters of business to matters concerned with the firm's interaction with government? Some executives say that attention has turned from the concerns of competitors, customers, suppliers, and internal operations to activities concerned with outwitting the government bureaucrat.

It is generally agreed in most industries that new regulations are putting a significant drag on productivity by diverting capital to nonproductive uses, by slowing research and development, and by prohibiting the use of efficient production processes. General Motors, for instance, employs about 24,000 people who report to various regulators. Consider the chemical industry where nearly one quarter of capital investment has been diverted to the purchase of pollution-abatement and other unproductive assets. A U.S. Department of Labor estimate shows that the billions invested for nonproducing pollution control, etc., cuts growth by 0.4% per year.

CAPITAL INVESTMENT

According to the Council of Economic Advisors, a major reason for the productivity decline is the weakness of fixed business investment over the past several years. In support of this contention, the Council offers statistics to show the decline of capital stock per unit of labor from an annual rate of 3% to 1.75%.

Certainly, capital investments and productivity are directly related. And the lack of capital is not the whole story. The age of a U.S. plant is 20 years—8 years older than the equivalent German plant and more than 10 years older than the equivalent Japanese facility. Figure 3-1 demonstrates graphically the poor record of the United States relative to that of other nations.

Several reasons (e.g., slack in existing capacity, diversion of funds to social services and environment, energy costs, inflation, uncertain climate for risk capital) have been advanced to explain this shortfall in capital investment. Not the least of these reasons is the declining savings rate and hence the availability of savings for investment. While the Japanese rate of savings as a share of after tax personal income is 25%, and West Germany saves at the rate of 17%, the U.S. rate has declined from 7.7% in 1975 to less than 4% in 1980. In 1980 Japan,

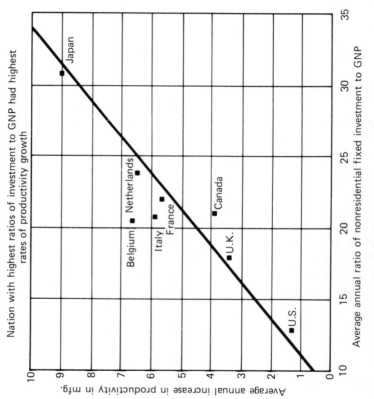

Nation with highest ratios of investment to GNP had highest rates of productivity growth

FIGURE 3-1. Investment and Productivity in U.S. and Other Industrial Nations, 1960-1976 (*Source:* U.S. Bureau of Labor Statistics and Organization for Economic Cooperation and Development).

54

with an economy half the size of ours, was spending more in absolute terms on plant and equipment than the United States.

CHANGING WORKER ATTITUDES

The complaints that "People don't want to work any-more" and that "Young people don't work like we did at their age," are probably the most *popular* explanations for low productivity. No less a person than Arthur Burns, then Chairman of the Board of Governors of the Federal Reserve System stated, "My own judgement is that we have been undergoing a change in our social values and attitudes that has contributed significantly to poorer job performance in recent years."

Many executives think that militant *labor unions* restrict improvement in productivity. No doubt, this thought has some validity. In some companies it appears that an imbalance of power between management and labor has occurred. In some extreme cases unions may have as much to say about day-to-day operations as management. One frustrated executive remarked, "Workers believe that since they come to the plant forty hours per week they can't be expected to work, too!"

Although the significant change in the labor force (i.e., more women, younger workers with less experience and training, shift to service workers) may account for part of the decline in productivity, there is no clear empirical evidence that a decline in the work ethic is also at fault. Even if there were a decline in the work ethic, the challenge represents an opportunity for managers everywhere.

SHIFT TO SERVICE ECONOMY

Service industries (e.g., retailing, health, travel, banking, education, insurance, government) are clearly outpacing manufacturing in growth. Already services employ more than twice as many people as do goods producers. And when you consider the large numbers of workers in "service" jobs (e.g., accounting, data processing, personnel, design, market research) within goods producing firms, it becomes evident that this sector is enormous.

So, the service sector is growing. What does this mean? It is frequently asserted that the opportunity for raising productivity is less for service workers than for production workers. This assertion appears to be doubtful on two counts. First, there is no statistical evidence to support a lesser productivity growth rate in services than in manufacturing. The exception to this may be office work where costs are expected to double over the next six years. Second, the opportunity for improvement seems to be at least as great in services as in any other sector of the economy. Again, this represents a challenge for the management process and for managers in the service sector.

OTHER CAUSES

Some other reasons, not as frequently advanced as those above, may nevertheless demonstrate a causal relationship with the decline of productivity.

Decline of Research and Development. Many studies have suggested that reduced research and development (R&D) expenditures—resulting from an apparent decline in Yankee ingenuity and innovation—is a reason for productivity decline. The conclusion of a two-day meeting held by the American Association for the Advancement of Science was as follows: "The United States is losing its competitive edge in technology because American industry is spending less on research and because the Federal Government withdrew much of its support for industrial research at the ends of the Apollo space program and the Vietnam War."

Other researchers conclude that although this relationship between R&D and productivity does exist, the "lag" between expenditures and application payoff is too long to explain the fairly recent precipitous drop in productivity. Moreover, the decline of R&D has been largely in federal government programs for defense and space, whose connection with productivity advances is slight at best. There is also evidence that the R&D financed by individual companies is turning more to short-term projects designed to meet regulatory requirements, rather than long-term projects with impacts on future productivity.

In summary, the reduction in R&D expenditures is probably not responsible for much of the *recent* retardation in productivity. This is not to say, of course, that continued and expanded R&D efforts should not be undertaken for future productivity and for projects that go to improve output per unit of input rather than those projects that add little or nothing to real output.

Inflation. Is the productivity decline caused partly by inflation or is it the other way around?* It is certain that *lower* results in productivity combined with *higher* wages can result only in inflation. Perhaps there is a "vicious circle" effect in operation.

To the extent that inflation results in increased *relative* cost of plant and equipment as compared to labor and the *relative* cost of operating capital, there can be little doubt that these investment *disincentives* are bad news. Inflation also tends to be a self-fulfilling prophecy; if

---

* Nobel laureate economist Milton Friedman stated that higher wages and the price-wage spiral are an *effect* of inflation, not a *cause*. See Milton and Rose Friedman, *Free to Choose: A Personal Statement* (Harcourt Brace Jovanovich, Inc., 1980).

people think it will happen, it will happen. This expectation is another disincentive for investment. The entire process has a tendency to substitute labor for capital.

Energy. The rise in energy costs has shocked the world economy, as well as each of us as individual investors and consumers. The impact of this price rise on productivity, however, is not clear.

Aside from the inflationary effects noted above, arising from the *cost* of energy, the mere rise in cost alone has little effect on productivity (output/input). For example, the "productivity" of a car's engine may be 18 miles/gallon (output/input) and remains at this ratio despite the price rise of gasoline. The cost of driving the car may rise, but the productivity of the engine does not change.

In business, however, the relationship is not so simple. Some economists argue that the rise in energy costs does have a negative effect on productivity. This effect results from the tendency to economize on energy by substituting the use of other resources, including labor. This substitution of labor for energy causes a reduction in the firm's capital/labor ratio, which in turn results in lower labor productivity. Other researchers say that this effect is minimal, and they cite statistics showing that energy used per unit of output has increased only about 4% over the amount normally expected *without* the price rise.

Lack of Programs. Few programs have been developed or implemented at the federal level to deal specifically with the problem of productivity decline. Aside from Reaganomics and "supply-side" efforts at monetary and fiscal policy, what can be done?

Federal government efforts could include those policies and/or programs designed to:

1. Improve incentives for improving labor skills, increasing the quantity and quality of plant, equipment, and research and development
and
2. Produce and use energy resources efficiently.

Furthermore, Washington could make some effort at programs targeted for increasing productivity. For example, the United States is the only major industrial power without substantial government sponsorship of *productivity centers*. Compare this, for example, with Japan. During the most recent period for which data are available, productivity in Japan increased at five times the rate in the United States. Japanese government expenditures on productivity improvement and productivity centers are over six times the amount spent by the U.S. government, despite the fact that our federal budget is five times larger than Japan's. Many other industrialized nations have government-sponsored productivity centers for the express purpose of conducting research and promoting a variety of productivity programs.

Lack of Goals. It is an axiom of management that without a goal, no plan is possible; "If you don't know where you're going, there's no way to get there." What is the goal of productivity improvement in the United States? To "do something" or "improve productivity?" These platitudes are as elusive as "contain inflation" or "do something about unemployment."

Until goals and objectives are set for productivity and related to other components of the economy, few specific action plans can be devised on a national basis to deal with the problem—or to turn the problem into an opportunity. Fortunately, the individual organization, public or private, can more easily set objectives for productivity improvement and get on with the necessary action plans to reach its objectives.

Summary: U.S. Productivity and Quality Circles

Earlier in this chapter we referred to the poor productivity record of the U.S. steel industry. Former productivity rates have been called "almost shameful" by top management in the industry. By 1981 this record had improved substantially—better personnel relations is the reason. Now better communications, worker involvement, and labor-management participation teams are among the innovations that have raised productivity, output, and profits. The steel industry accomplished this, not with expenditures for capital equipment, but with management and workers working together, by encouraging workers to use their brains as well as their labor. The conclusion emerges that if the steel industry can do it, everyone can.

Objectives, plans, procedures, and reports don't get results; only *people* do. It becomes clear then that a major route to increased productivity is the better use of people by providing opportunities for them to participate in decisions made about their work. For nonsupervisory employees, the vehicle for achieving this participation is the quality circle.

Aside from the intangible benefits of QC membership, there is a hidden gold mine containing billions of dollars in potential productivity improvements. All we have to do is mine this potential.

4

Quality Circles and Productivity

The productivity of people requires that people are constantly challenged to think through what they can do to improve what they are already doing. Above all, it requires willingness to ask employees and to listen to their answers.

PETER DRUCKER

In chapter 1 we summarized the benefits of quality circles as reported by a selected group of 24 facilitators in as many companies representing a variety of industries. To repeat, these reported benefits were ranked as follows:

- Improved Communications
- Job Satisfaction
- Improved Morale
- Productivity Improvement (other than cost savings)
- Quality Improvement
- Cost Savings

The secondary ranking of so-called "bottom-line" benefits (i.e., productivity, quality, cost) does not, of course, suggest that these are any less important than the *behavioral* or personnel relations dimension. Rather, it is widely assumed that if conditions surrounding job satisfaction are upgraded, productivity improvement will follow. At any rate, improved productivity is a major objective of quality circles.

In a 1981 study of 16 major companies with successful productivity programs, Chicago consulting firm, A. T. Kearney, Inc., found that these companies earned 30% to 38% more on sales than others in the industry. Fully 96% of these companies ranked people involvement as one of the basic keys to success. They all used a "bottom-up" instead of a "top-down" approach in establishing a participatory environment.

Quality Circle Potential

The Kearney report mentioned above also concluded: "There is a $380 billion additional profit opportunity available to American industry." Another executive who suggests productivity improvement through worker involvement is Lewis H. Young, editor-in-chief of *Business Week*. As he sees it, "The question for American business is how to get those productivity increases without shutting down all our plants or investing a lot in new machinery, automatic devices and computer systems. One way is to give workers some say in how they do their jobs." Giving workers some say may begin with changing from a classical management style to a productivity management style, as discussed in the following.

THE ICEBERG ANALOGY

We know that approximately 90% of an iceberg's volume is under water and hidden from the observer's view. Only a small portion is visible. To the uninformed traveler, only the visible portion seems to exist. However, a seasoned sailor seeks to account for the hidden part below the surface.

An organization is somewhat like an iceberg (see figure 4-1). The novice, or the seat-of-the-pants manager, sees only visible organizational potential and usually adopts a managerial style that is heavily dependent on tradition and personal experience. He likes to describe himself as "informal" and feels that popular management techniques are nothing more than commonsense descriptions of what he does instinctively. He runs things "by the book" and depends on formal authority and standard procedures. He is the classical manager.

What the classical manager frequently overlooks is the unreleased potential in the organization for improved productivity through more modern management methods. If he could visualize the potential for improved productivity, both he and the organization would benefit.

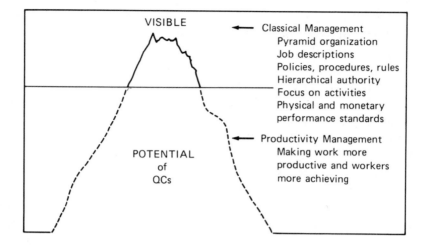

FIGURE 4-1. The organization as an iceberg.

The potential for improved productivity—the submerged portion of the iceberg—is significant but is being suppressed by classical techniques of organization and management. The way to releasing this potential lies in adopting a systems approach to managing productivity, and a major component of the system is the work force.

TEAM ORGANIZATIONS

The real organizational problem, at least at the level of the front-line supervisor or middle manager, is to balance the existing functional structure with its skill specialization against the organization of people and tasks necessary to achieve results—to "break through" the pyramid, so to speak. The answer to this paradox appears to lie in the team approach to organization style. This approach complements the classical structure of functional grouping (the employee's "home") with a work team (the employee's "place of work"). Committees, expediters, departmental meetings, and the like are not

teams. The team organization is not a temporary expe-
dient to solve a special short-run problem. It involves a
design principle all its own.

The team form of organization is not new. The task
force and the project manager have been around for
years. IBM, for example, has always encouraged workers
to form teams within the mass-production system. But
the use of teams is growing. The automobile industry has
been experimenting on the assembly line. The use of
product managers and project managers is growing
increasingly popular in industry.

The venture team concept is a recent innovation
developed to meet the demand for a breakthrough in
product design and marketing. At Texas Instruments,
team management is a way of life and has been carried to
a high degree of sophistication. Several hundred
"TAPs"—tactical action programs—were organized to
achieve company strategy and goals. Motorola has
pushed decentralization down to the plant level where
product managers develop their own strategy and product plans. Ralston Purina has local decision-making work
groups right on the shop floor to innovate in work standards and methods. A few companies have organized
"productivity teams."

The team approach to organization style offers the
front-line supervisor and middle manager, whether line
or staff, an alternative to the classical structure, or
rather, a modification to it in order to achieve productivity. However, the team approach is not a panacea nor
does it apply in all situations. It is not generally appropriate by itself, but must be complementary to the existing structure. QCs achieve this.

What Is Productivity?

There is now almost universal agreement that the primary job of a manager is to create a whole that is larger
than the sum of its parts, an organizational entity that

turns out more than the sum of the resources put into it. In business this is termed *profit.* In the public sector it may be called *surplus.* All organizations must add some value to the inputs they receive. Likewise, individual managers must add value to the resources that are placed into their custody for processing into outputs. Quality circles can help.

THE ORGANIZATIONAL SYSTEM

Consider the concept of an organizational *system,* shown in figure 4-2. The system (organization or company) consists of three components:

- *Inputs.* Money, human resources, materials, machines and other fixed assets, technology, and information.
- *Activities.* Design, manufacturing, selling, servicing, etc.
- *Output.* A result.

The organization (or subsystem, department, individual) receives inputs, *adds value* to get an output—a result.

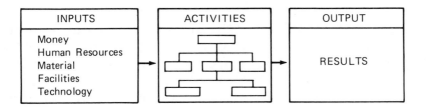

FIGURE 4-2. The organizational system.

Let me repeat. The organization (subsystem, department, individual) receives inputs and adds value to get an output —a result!

$$\text{The ratio } \frac{OUTPUT}{INPUT} \text{ is productivity!}$$

$$\text{Let me repeat. The ratio } \frac{OUTPUT}{INPUT} \text{ is productivity!}$$

Needless to say, if the ratio $\frac{\text{Output}}{\text{Input}}$ is not a positive number, the organization or department is in trouble. It is not "earning its way."

THE CONCEPT OF ADDED VALUE: RESULTS

Added value, in the case of the entire company, the division, or the profit center, includes all the costs of all the efforts of the organizational entity and the entire reward received for these efforts. It accounts for all the resources the business itself contributes to the final product and the appraisal of the efforts of the business by the market. Hence, in many aspects, the added value can be called a result.

While it is easy to compute the result of the entire organization with such ratios or measures of $\frac{\text{Output}}{\text{Input}}$ as $\frac{\text{Return}}{\text{Investment}}$ (return on investment) or $\frac{\text{Profit}}{\text{Sales}}$ (profit on sales), it is not easy for the single department or individual to define the *result* of the department or individual effort. A worker may perform to a standard (result) of 2.1 units per man-hour, but what is the result, standard, or productivity ratio for market research, computer programming, design engineering, or training?

The difficulty of defining and measuring the productivity ratio $\frac{\text{Output}}{\text{Input}}$, which we shall call *result*, is evident and lies at the bottom of much of the difficulty of measuring and improving productivity. You cannot very well plan to improve something you can't measure or define. And yet the overwhelming majority of people in an organization *cannot define the result expected from their job* in terms of value added. They insist on thinking of their job in terms of *input* or *activity* rather than results. Despite the simplicity of the INPUT/ACTIVITY/OUTPUT concept of productivity, many managers continue to focus on input or activity, sometimes with total disregard for results!

In summary, PRODUCTIVITY is:

Effectiveness not efficiency
The ratio between what you put in for what you get out (Result)

$$\text{Making the ratio } \frac{\text{OUTPUT}}{\text{INPUT}} \text{ get bigger}$$

Five Ways to Improve Productivity

At this point it should be rather clear that productivity is a *ratio* concept. Improvement means making the ratio bigger—the ratio of the output of goods and services produced divided by the input used to produce them. Hence, the ratio can be made bigger either by increasing the output, reducing the input, or both.

Historically, productivity improvement has focused on technology and capital to reduce the input of *labor* cost of production. Output was generally thought to be subject to improvement by getting more production through the application of industrial engineering techniques such as methods analysis, workflow, and so on.

Both of these approaches—increasing the output or reducing the input—are still appropriate, but to a much lesser degree. The movement today is toward better use of the potential available through human resources. Each worker can be his or her own industrial engineer—a mini-manager, so to speak. This potential can be tapped by allowing and encouraging people to innovate in one or more of the five ways described below.

REDUCE COSTS

$$\frac{-}{\downarrow} \quad \frac{\text{Output Same}}{\text{Input Down}}$$

Without a doubt, cost reduction is the traditional and most widely used approach to productivity improvement. This item from an American Standard Company newsletter is typical of this type of program:

In this inflationary environment we have no alternative but to increase our productivity —in other words, to reduce our costs per unit of output. Only by doing so can we maintain the profitability that enables us to provide products for our customers, dividends for our stockholders, and jobs for our employees.

Cost reduction is, of course, a very appropriate route to improving productivity. However, many companies maintain a somewhat outdated "across-the-board" mentality that results in mandates for everyone to "cut expenses by 10%." Frequently, staff services are slashed. Training is reduced, and the result is an inefficient sales force, reduced advertising, loss of market share, reduced R&D. The result is a noncompetitive product; maintenance is delayed and machine downtime is increased, secretarial help is cut, and highly paid executives type their own letters.

Under this "management by drive" approach, people are perceived as a direct expense, and the immediate route to cost reduction is seen as cutting this expense as much as possible. Almost always, this policy leads to employee resentment. This in turn leads to resistance, slowdown, and in some cases sabotage. The "rate-buster" is universally resented because everyone, worker and union alike, is concerned about spreading the work. Naturally, management's efforts to cut back are resisted.

This "panic" or "crisis" approach to cost reduction is frequently counterproductive. It may result in trading today's headache for tomorrow's upset stomach as in this example:

The chairperson of International Harvester, a disciple of cost cutting, saved $460 million in two years and cut 11,000 jobs from the company payroll. Earnings were boosted by 98%. But when he chose to engage the powerful United Auto Workers in his cost-cutting crusade, the result was a strike that idled 36% of the work force. Neither he nor the union would yield on union work rules concerning overtime. The impact was devastating. At last report, market share was down, dealers were unhappy due to parts shortages, capital expansion was delayed, product innovation was put off, earnings were reduced, and the customer base was eroding.

For a more positive approach to cost reduction, consider these examples:

Hughes Aircraft Company is in an industry that spends huge sums on R&D, most frequently to produce technical specifications without adequate consideration of manufacturing costs. The company's present policy is to encourage cost reduction by designing for ease of manufacturing, an approach to productivity that is overlooked by many design engineers.

At Aluminum Company of America (Alcoa), where management approaches productivity with almost a religious fervor, improvements are attributed to a 50/50 split between better work-force utilization and capital investment. In the Mill Products Division, a centralized material-handling group in a major plant was decentralized. Resulting job combinations and practice changes reduced numbers of employees needed by 20%, or 55 people. No capital was expended.

MANAGE GROWTH

$$\frac{\uparrow}{\uparrow} \quad \frac{\text{Output Up}}{\text{Input Up by Lesser Amount}}$$

Growth without productivity improvement is FAT!

In this approach to improvement, an investment or *cost addition* is made that will return more than the cost of the investment, thus making the *ratio bigger*. Capital and technological improvements, systems design, training, organization design, and development are among the many ways to manage growth. These are particularly important to organizations whose sales and production are increasing. Some examples are these:

Many firms have achieved excellent results by applying electronics technology in process control, information systems, and related applications. The big movement of computer activity in manufacturing is through materials requirement planning (MRP), the growing component of an overall computerized manufacturing control system. Its purpose is to improve productivity by enabling a shop to react on a weekly or daily basis to changes in the master schedule, bill of materials, and labor costs, or to permit greater productivity levels with existing inputs.

At Burger King, computer readout terminals were installed in kitchens. Incoming orders entered into the computerized cash register out front are flashed on the screen in proper order. The cooks make fewer mistakes and don't waste so much food. Equally important, one manager states, "The demand at peak hours is so great that if we can produce more we can sell more. We have to do it in a very tight time frame. Nobody cares how many hamburgers we can make between 11:00 P.M. and 6 A.M."

In 1790, a census clerk with a pencil could process about 30 items a minute. In the 1980 census, the computers handled about 45 million items of information in the same time.

This approach does not necessarily mean additional investment in capital or methods improvement for it can also mean reducing the amount of input per unit of output during growth periods. This may be termed "cost avoidance."

At Corning Glass, energy is a substantial part of product cost. At the company's Glass Works, energy costs were $18 million in 1972. Between 1972 and 1979 the price of energy rose, but so did Corning's production volume. If this volume had been the same in 1979 as in 1972, the energy bill would have been $80 million. Instead, since production volume had increased, the company paid only $56 million for energy.

WORK SMARTER

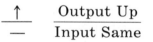

Working smarter means more output from the same input, thus allowing increases in sales or production at the same gross input and lower unit cost. We witness cases of this in attempts to "freeze" employment or budgets while expecting a higher level of activity. This mentality or approach is a short-run stopgap measure; it is hardly a rational course of action to improve productivity over the longer haul.

Better ways of making this ratio *bigger* might be getting more output by reducing manufacturing cost through product design, or getting more production from the same level of raw materials—increasing raw-materials turnover.

In one IBM plant, most employees were trained in methods analysis and improvement. The results were outstanding. Suggestions for improvements accepted by the company went from 500 to 2,600. Three out of four employees *turned in suggestions, and improvements over $1 million were clearly identified.*

At Burger King, "the company that is run by 50,000 teenagers," a Drive-Through Task Force computed that it took 11 seconds to react after a car drove over the bell hose that announced the car's arrival at the drive-in window. The "productivity experts" moved the hose back 10 feet, so that by the time a car had braked, the order taker was waiting to scribble down the customer's order.

PARE DOWN

$$\downarrow \quad \frac{\text{Output Down}}{\downarrow \quad \text{Input Down More}}$$

Paring down is similar to cost reduction, except that in this case sales or production is off but input should be reduced by a larger amount, thus making the *ratio bigger.*

This productivity improvement can frequently be achieved through "sloughing off." Marginal or unproductive facilities, employees, customers, products, or activities are candidates to be "sloughed off." In most organizations, there are many more opportunities than are generally realized. To quote Peter Drucker, "Most plans concern themselves only with the new and additional things that have to be done—new products, new processes, new markets, and so on. But the key to doing something different tomorrow is getting rid of the no-longer-productive, the obsolescent, the obsolete."

In an article entitled "Getting By Without a Tin Cup," Fortune *magazine reports that U.S. Steel chairman David M. Roderick has announced that he is prepared to take a hard line on rising labor costs and falling productivity. Just before Christmas, Roderick announced the closing of 16 plants and other facilities in several states.*

The action was a calculated move to weed out uneconomic facilities.

WORK EFFECTIVELY

$$\frac{\uparrow}{\downarrow} \quad \frac{\text{Output Up}}{\text{Input Down}}$$

In this, the most effective of all approaches to productivity improvement, we can get more for less.

Crompton Company is a New York–based manufacturer of corduroy and velveteen in the highly competitive textile industry, where it is not unusual for 10% of finished cloth to be defective and sold for 30¢ on the dollar. Crompton knows that the overriding ingredient in this business is people, and through people involvement has managed to hold rejects to under 4% while sales are increasing.

Visual Graphics, a Fort Lauderdale company that manufactures high-quality industrial cameras, has been experiencing rapid growth accompanied by new and modified products. The company was able to reduce unit cost in the face of rising raw-material cost by value analysis, product design, and production scheduling.

Quality Circles and the Bottom Line

The payoff from relatively small increases in productivity can have a disproportionate and positive effect on both operating margins and net profits—the bottom line. Consider that by eliminating one nonproductive hour in a day for each worker you can increase work-force productivity by 20%. Gains of up to 25% as a result of using employees as an intelligent resource are not uncommon. With payroll costs running on the average at about eight times net profit, the potential is great.

At Texas Instruments, where productivity improvement is a way of life, productivity growth has averaged 15% per year for the last 10 years. This has resulted in a unit labor output more than three times as great as previously.

In one U.S. Navy West Coast shipyard, serious problems were encountered with too high costs, low productivity, leave abuse, and high turnover. Following an incentive productivity improvement program, productivity improved by 18%, and overtime and backlog were eliminated.

Consider a hypothetical case of a firm that makes an operating profit of 4%—$4 per $100 of sales. In order to increase profits by $1, to $5, it is necessary to increase sales to $125, *a sales increase of 25%.* However, if the company could cut costs by only 1%, it would make the same increased profit of $1—*the same as increasing sales by 25%.* Now ask yourself which alternative is easier and more logical—*increasing sales by 25% or improving productivity by 1%?* Most managers continue to think that increased sales is the primary route to the bottom line.

The 10 Percent Leverage

In seminars and conversations with over a thousand supervisors, we have asked these questions: "Do you think that you could achieve an improvement of *10%* in the cost or output of your job? Are you willing to commit yourself to this improvement?"

In well over 90% of the cases, we have found that the supervisor or worker involved will reply: "No problem," or "Sure, I can do it," or a similar answer followed by a commitment to achieve the *10%* improvement. Many will "sign up" for 20%, some for 30%.

What would happen to the bottom line if through the use of quality circles or other productivity efforts the company could improve productivity by 10%? Many people think that profits would go up by an equivalent amount (10%). But the leverage effect is much greater.

To demonstrate the *leverage* of such improvement, we have taken the composite financial income statement (P&L) of over 100 firms of the Fortune 500 (see table 4-1). The bottom line is 6% of sales. (The all-industry composite of 1,200 companies was 5.1%, ranging from 1.1% for 25 companies in the automotive industry to 10.4% for 27 companies in the office equipment and computer industry.)

Column 1 of Table 4-1 indicates the actual financial results for the full year. Column 2 shows what the results would be if *operating* costs were reduced by 10% while sales remained the same. The results are impressive. If the 10% improvement could be achieved, the bottom line

TABLE 4-1
Composite Income Statement (P&L) Demonstrating the Leverage Effect of a 10% Improvement in Productivity (As a Percentage of Sales)

	Actual	After 10% Productivity Improvement
SALES	100	100
Cost of Sales		
Material	30	27
Labor	18	16
Overhead	23	21
G & A	23	21
TOTAL	94	85
PROFIT	6	15

would increase by approximately 150%. Obviously the potential gains from minor productivity improvements are impressive.

Measuring Productivity

Management writer Peter Drucker tells us, "Without productivity objectives, a business does not have direction. Without productivity measurements, it does not have control." A prerequisite to any productivity improvement effort is the establishment of a system of measurements through which an organization can determine its level of productivity and compare it against its own past performance, the experience of similar firms, and others in the industry. Measures form the basis upon which action plans for improvement can be made.

Despite the importance of measures, useful techniques for establishing them are not widely available. Certainly the brief discussion in this chapter must, of necessity, be cursory. In introducing the topic of measurement, we wish to emphasize the importance of simplicity. The advantages of complexity are few; the advantages of simplicity are many. The cardinal rule in measurement is *Keep it Simple!* Our discussion is confined to:

- Total Factor Productivity
- Partial Factor Productivity
- Functional and/or Departmental Measures
- Individual Measures
- Industry Measures

TOTAL FACTOR PRODUCTIVITY

This is the broadest measure of output to input and can be expressed thus:

Total Productivity

$$= \frac{\text{Total Output}}{\text{Total Input}}$$

$$= \frac{\text{Total Output}}{\text{Labor} + \text{Materials} + \text{Energy} + \text{Capital}}$$

It is significant to the state of productivity measurement that the government doesn't even compile total productivity figures, since the measurement problems are immense. A variety of public sources, such as the Bureau of Labor Statistics' *Output per Employee and Output per Employee-Hour*, are available for macroeconomic measures. However, these ratios consider only the efficiency of using human resources and thus are partial productivity measures. Total factor productivity is not only concerned with how many units are produced or how many letters are typed but also considers all aspects of producing goods and services. Hence, this measure is concerned with the efficiency of the entire plant or company.

One innovative approach to measuring total factor productivity has been designed by the Texas Hospital Association for measuring the performance of hospitals of varying sizes and complexity. Output *is defined as the synthesized case, covering the time from patient admission to discharge.* Inputs *comprise* labor *(wages, benefits, etc.) and* nonlabor *costs. This system of total factor productivity allows the hospital administrator to perform productivity and cost analysis over time and against other hospitals of like size.*

PARTIAL PRODUCTIVITY

Partial productivity measures are established by developing ratios of total output to one or more input categories, and can be expressed thus:

$$\text{Partial Productivity} = \frac{\text{Total Output}}{\text{Partial Input}}$$

$$\text{Labor Productivity} = \frac{\text{Total Output}}{\text{Labor Input}}$$

$$\text{Material Productivity} = \frac{\text{Total Output}}{\text{Material Input}}$$

and so on for capital and energy.

All measures are ratios of $\frac{\text{Output}}{\text{Input}}$ *quantities.* Although some ratios can be expressed in quantitative terms such as "units produced per man-hour," others must combine unlike *quantities:* tons and gallons of products; employee-hours; pounds, kwhs, etc., of inputs. To solve this problem, a set of weights representative of the relative importance of the various items can be used to combine unlike quantities. Base-period prices are the recommended weights to be used for total productivity calculation, although other weighting systems such as "man-hour equivalents" can be used.

You can determine the relative change in quantities from the base period to the current period by summing the current quantities and multiplying this figure by their respective weights, then dividing the same weights by the sum of the base-period quantities. This calculation is performed separately for the outputs and the inputs. The output/input ratio results in the relative change in productivity from the base to the current period.

Labor, broadly defined as the contribution of all organizational members, is usually a pivotal input to measure. This is logical. The labor input is not only a substantial cost of producing output, but it is through the *people* input that we achieve optimum use of the other inputs of capital, material, and energy.

At Texas Instruments, a company that successfully uses productivity measurement principles, a People Effectiveness Index (PEI) *has been devised. It is calculated by dividing net sales billed by total payroll plus payroll-related benefits. This index gives a measurement of productivity improvement, takes into account decreases in prices and increases in wages and benefits, and is easily calculated using two figures that appear in each annual report. Return on assets (ROA) is the conventional performance measurement derived by dividing net after-tax income by the average assets employed during the year. Combining the PEI with the ROA yields the profit-sharing percentage, an excellent measure of overall productivity growth.*

FUNCTIONAL AND DEPARTMENTAL MEASURES

The productivity coordinator of a major electrical manufacturer had this to say: "A company is much more likely to benefit from the detailed monitoring of key departments and activities than from an effort to apply comprehensive, companywide coverage."

Most firms rely largely on budgetary dollar accounting data to analyze their operations, even though these data include the effects of inflation, tax, depreciation, and somewhat arbitrary accounting-cost allocations. Frequently these data are not significantly related to the process under study. It is desirable, therefore, to develop measures that reflect output and input in more realistic terms. Where financial measures are used, it is appropriate to deflate them as described above.

It is impractical here to list the many functions and departments of the typical company and the several measures that could be devised for each. The sampling listed below should be sufficiently detailed to encourage individuals to develop their own functional or departmental measure(s).

Function	Measure
Customer Support	Cost per field technician, cost per warranty callback, service cost per unit shipped
Data Processing	Computer instructions per program, computer operations employees per systems design employees, data-processing expense to company expense, data-processing expense per CPU hour
Quality Assurance	Units returned for warranty repair as a percentage of units shipped
Design	Drafting time per original drawing, drawing error rate
Materials Storage	Parts picking time, storage per square foot, stockout rate
Order Processing*	Orders processed per employee, sales per order-processing employee
Personnel	Rate of offers accepted, hires per recruiter, department expense to total company expense
Production Control	Inventory turnover rate, items in inventory to items not moved in 12 months, order cycle time, machine utilization, total production to production schedule
Plant Engineering	Drawings produced to number of draftsmen, drawings produced to design engineering staff
Receiving	Volume handled to unloading man-hours, receipts per workday
Shipping	Orders shipped on time, demurrage charges to total nonlabor expense, packing expense to total shipping expenses
Testing	Man-hours per run-hour, test-equipment calibration time, test expense to rework expense

*One company computed that it cost $5 to process an order. Since profit on sales was 5% and half the orders were under $100, a new pricing policy became evident: "No orders under $75."

INDIVIDUAL MEASURES

Productivity measures, just like standards of performance, offer the individual manager and the worker alike guidelines for responsible action, and open the way to increased productivity.

To the fullest extent possible, a measure should always be designed to be specific and quantitative. It should be as clear as *par* on the golf course. A golfer can go out on the course alone or with a foursome, but when the eighteenth hole is reached, the player knows just how good a golfer he or she is and how much improvement is needed. Indeed, the golfer is aware of achievement as the game unfolds—it is not necessary to await the finish.

Perhaps the easiest and most effective way to set standards is to list the responsibilities of the job on a piece of paper, then list the measures (results expected) that would indicate that the job is being performed satisfactorily. For example:

Responsibility	Measure
Maintenance	Maintain an uptime machine rate of 94%.
Assembly	Maintain production schedule to actual production at 90%.
Accounts Receivable	Maintain an accounts-receivable level at 42 days.
Computer Programming	Write computer programs on time and to customer specifications.

Having established these measures, or standards, the individual can then write a *productivity improvement objective* (results expected). Following the format suggested below, these measures could be written:

My productivity improvement objective is

Action Verb	Results Expected	Time	Cost
To Improve	machine uptime from 94% to 97%	by June 30	at no increase in manpower or preventive maintenance costs.

Action Verb	Results Expected	Time	Cost
To Increase	actual production from 90% of schedule to 95%	in the remainder of year	at the same cost of manufacture and product quality.
To Improve	cash flow by 10% and reduce A/R level to 36 days	by May 31	within existing budget, personnel, and equipment.
To Avoid	program and system retrofit expense by debugging program	prior to second system test	in no additional time or reduction in programs written.

A final note on individual measures is the caution to pay careful attention to employee perceptions of their evaluation. If the measure is "laid on" or is perceived as a formal and critical evaluation, the person may "play it safe" by working on sure things or focusing only on the activities that are being measured.

The obvious answer is to encourage people to develop their own measures. This is especially appropriate in staff or white-collar jobs, in which measuring productivity is so difficult.

Occidental Life Insurance Company in California installed a productivity improvement program which set up flexible working hours, shortened summer workweeks to 4½ days, and let employees establish their own output goals. "Take a person who's been running a family — planning, organizing, and controlling — and it doesn't make sense to suppress those capabilities during the working day," commented the vice president of personnel. "It's hard to measure productivity in an insurance company.

*That's why it's important to get employees involved in set-
ting their own objectives."*

INDUSTRY MEASURES

A productivity measurement is not only the best
yardstick for comparing different divisions, units, and
profit centers within the same multidivisional company,
it also provides an excellent way to compare the management of different companies within the same industry.
All businesses have access to pretty much the same resources. The only thing that differentiates one business
from another in the same industry is the quality of their
management. We measure this quality by the degree to
which resources (inputs) are utilized.

Comparing your firm with others in the same industry:

- Provides a benchmark for you to gauge your productivity change in relation to the industry.
- Provides the trigger for an analysis of different
ways to implement productivity change.
- Can be an aid in forecasting trends and patterns.
- Indicates specific improvement potentials in
major productivity inputs.

Measuring Quality Circles

Despite the unanimity of opinion that some framework of
measures is essential for a productivity improvement
program, there is less than widespread agreement on
whether quality circles should be measured and if so,
how.

Those opposed to measurement (a minority) take the
view that measures tend to take on the nature of stan-

dards, controls, variance reporting, and the other trappings of management direction and checks. It is feared that this approach will inhibit the freedom of discussion and the expression of opinion so necessary in QC sessions. In short, when measurement is used, the program may be perceived as a management, rather than as a worker, program.

In an effort to determine how measures were used in actual corporate practice, we surveyed 24 companies that had significant experience with the process. Company facilitators were asked: "Do you believe that the effectiveness of quality circles should be measured: ( ) always, ( ) most of the time, ( ) some of the time, or ( ) not at all?" In order of frequency of response, the replies were:

Reply	Number Responding
Always	8
Most of the time	4
Some of the time	9
Not at all	3
Total	24

Based on the foregoing responses, it appears that industry practice approves measurement at least some of the time. This supports our conclusion. We believe that progress must be measured from some benchmark—some measure. Without this you don't know where you're going or where you've been.

WHY MEASURE QUALITY CIRCLES?

The same survey asked company quality circle facilitators to "prioritize [rank] your reasons for measuring the effect of quality circles." In order of frequency of response (priority), the replies were:

Reply	Respondents Ranking It		Overall Rank (Weighted Average)
	First	Second	
To direct circle activity in the most productive way	7	3	1
To sell management on initial or continued circle support	5	6	2
To "keep score" for QC members as feedback	7	4	3
To choose between alternative problems		3	4
To sell management on approving the recommendations of circles	3	3	5
Because management expects it	2	2	6
To calculate incentive or rewards for circles		3	7

HOW ARE QUALITY CIRCLES MEASURED?

In an attempt to determine what kind of measures were used for circle activity, the above survey asked a question regarding the types of measures used in the individual companies. The responses are summarized below:

Measure(s) Used	Number of Companies Using	Ranking (Weighted Average)
Functional and/or Departmental	12	1
Individual Circle Measure	11	2
Partial Factor (labor, material, capital, energy)	9	3
Total Factor	5	4
Industry Measures	4	5
White-collar Productivity	3	6

5

Quality Circles and the Human Dimension

Never underestimate management's ability to mismanage.

ROBERT E. COLE, Director
Center for Japanese Studies,
University of Michigan

Companies that are truly determined to develop managers with professional skills in working with people might well heed the lessons of the 1960s and 1970s. During that period, scores of companies enthusiastically sent their managers to the "charm schools" of sensitivity training (T-Group), conflict resolution encounter groups, and the like. The well-intentioned but nonetheless naive goal was to turn these managers into expert person-to-person communicators and "nice guys" overnight. Thus, it was assumed they would then be receptive to participative management when they returned to the company.

But T-Groups and such do not seem to be the "in" thing at the moment. Their track record has not been too impressive in changing managerial behavior. Those managers whose attitudes did change all too often returned to unchanged workplaces, where peer pressure, as well as the economic and promotional reward systems, caused them to revert to their old authoritarian management styles. A recurring complaint among middle managers returning from these training sessions was the uphill battle they encountered in trying to implement the knowledge and skills they had learned. Many times the complaint was, "Top management should take these courses so they would understand what we're trying to do."

This has led to the dilemma of how to convince top management of the need for further training of middle-level managers. Top management will say, "We've had training in the company for years. Our middle managers have had sensitivity training (or organizational development, human resources development, etc.) for several years." The problem here is that the "trained" managers interact, if at all, with their peer group rather than using this expertise with the supervisory group and the workers.

So—what is the answer? How can a "style of management" using professional methods be developed to produce results in today's modern industry?

There is an old comedy routine used for years on the "Fibber McGee and Molly" radio program which always brought a roar of delight from the audience. As Fibber opens his closet door, the contents pour forth and crash around him in utter disarray and confusion. Many executives view their organizations in this way. As the door to the "problems" closet is opened, out tumbles a disorganized array of functional crises brought on by subordinates who can't, or won't, work together. The executives wonder how to make a "system" of the mess.

Somewhat less in disarray, but nevertheless confusing, is the state-of-the-art in the "science" of organization and management. It is the intent of this chapter to bring the pieces together into a system. This integration is necessary because it is a fundamental premise of this book that the process of management must be clearly understood before major inroads can be made in productivity. Upon this understanding stands or falls the installation of quality circles as a process of management.

Motivation and the Work Force

Work and its role in people's lives has intrigued humans from time immemorial. It has occupied the minds of rulers, philosophers, poets, theologians, and scientists. Depending upon the time and the culture, work has been viewed as a punishment, a moral obligation, a means of salvation, an economic necessity, and a means of personal growth and self-fulfillment. The crucial determinant of how work is perceived is whether it is called a *task* (activity necessary for economic survival), an *occupation* (that which occupies much of people's time and effort), *employment* (that which uses skills towards some social or economic purpose), *vocation* (that which one is called to do), *mission* (that which one is called upon or sent to do), or *job* (that which one agrees or contracts to do).

These terms are used interchangeably, but there is a growing awareness that work may possess qualities that encompass all of them and yet go a step beyond. That step—that extra dimension—is self-expression or realization of one's innate potential to develop and to grow, to achieve and to create.

Industry has always addressed itself to the nature, function, organization, objectives, and design of work. While the human factor has undoubtedly influenced management's thinking and its planning of work, management's effort has been largely directed toward people's adaptation to technological and production requirements. Many industries have been reluctant to consider the creative potential of their workers.

Organizations don't have objectives—people do. Organizations don't achieve productivity—people do. An organization is nothing more than the combined efforts of the people who are its members. Despite this obvious truth, many managers hesitate to delegate or allow people to participate in decisions affecting them and the company. Jerome Rosow, President, Work in America Institute, described it succinctly when he stated: "Deep in his gut the American manager thinks people aren't important to productivity, that it's just a question of more capital or new technology. He's got to learn that people are the key and that we've got to unleash the untapped talent of workers."

THE WORK FORCE OF THE 1980S

It is widely agreed among successful and profitable firms that the greatest potential for increasing productivity lies in the motivation and the untapped abilities of the work force. Even the economic experts concerned with productivity indicate that in the years ahead improvements will derive even more from investment in human capital than from investment in plant and equipment.

Increasing numbers of company, union, and academic authorities are coming to believe that a new manager/worker relationship must include three basic elements:

1. The development of a nonadversarial relationship on the shop floor. With such a relationship, workers and bosses can collaborate on means and methods of production by circumventing adversarial procedures, such as grievance mechanisms. This need not violate union contracts or prevent unions from negotiating wages and benefits. Certainly, greater cooperation at the production level will involve workers in the business to a much greater extent.

2. A reform of bargaining, based on a mutuality of interests developed on the shop floor. This work-level cooperation might well slip over into the bargaining process, particularly if unions—reflecting the concerns of their members—tie themselves more tightly to the success of the individual company, rather than try to keep up with national wage patterns and outdo other unions.

3. A thoroughgoing change in management style in which the traditional top-to-bottom hierarchical form of decision making is replaced with a participation process. Decisions should be pushed to ever-lower levels, thereby encouraging employees, by extension, to become involved in the business itself. But this would also mean that management must share information with workers, divide with them the gains resulting from increased participation, and work much harder to provide job security and to prevent the catastrophic blows of unexpected plant shutdowns.

Even unions, historically concerned with little more than pay and benefits, are now adopting policies regarding quality circles as these relate to motivation and participation. Quoted here is a portion of a recent policy statement by the United Automobile Workers (UAW):

> Achieving job satisfaction includes not only decent working conditions, it must move to a higher plateau where the worker is not merely the adjunct of the tool, but in which he participates in the decision-making process which concerns his welfare on the job. This calls for a departure from the miniaturization and oversimplification of the jobs, symbolic of "scientific management," to a system which embraces broader distribution of authority, increasing rather than diminishing responsibility, combined with the engineering of more interesting jobs, with the opportunity to exercise a meaningful measure of autonomy and to utilize more varied skills. It requires tapping the creative and innovative ingenuity of the worker and his direct participation in the decisions involved in his job.

The modern manager must consider not only what is right for the company but what is right for the individual as well. In the past we have ordinarily considered these two requirements as conflicting. The problem now is to combine them into a single approach that meets the needs of the company as well as its personnel. It can be done.

Employees are no longer content with the traditional rewards offered by the company or by labor unions, such as more pay, four-day work weeks, more fringe benefits, and so on. What they really want is deep human satisfaction from their work. Managers should view this not as a problem but as an opportunity. In this chapter we will examine those factors which affect productivity and relate them to modern motivational philosophy and practice. This type of "results management" motivates the manager and the subordinate to action because each

decides what work is necessary to get the results de-
manded of human action, behavior, and motivation.

Peter Drucker wrote in 1939, "Any workable social
order such as the corporation must confer status and
function upon all its members." Apparently it has taken
40 years for this advice to catch on because today's
manager has come to realize that status and function
must be accommodated if the worker is to be productive
and achieving.

Management: Past versus Future

The first study of professional management and job design is generally considered to have begun near the
beginning of the twentieth century with the movement
toward mass-production and assembly-line operations.
Frederick W. Taylor's "work measurement" studies, and
those of his successors, Frank and Lillian Gilbreth, were
task-oriented. They emphasized fractionalization of
labor, techniques to improve efficiency, and "time-and-
motion" studies. These gave birth to engineered labor
standards, job-evaluation systems, piecework incentives,
and specialized skills training for mass-production operations. All the study, analysis, and work improvement effort was directed at the task and not at the social or personal needs of the individuals performing it.

Through this "scientific management" approach,
each step of production was to be reduced to its simplest
components and arranged in sequence to ensure the
highest level of productivity. Jobs were to be uniform and
specialized. Judgement, discretion, and skills were to be
minimized. Thus, the very process of production was to be
removed from the province of workers. The solution to
quality control, for example, was to be mechanical—a
system of inspectors combined with random sampling
making it no longer necessary for workers to think. As a
result, the American worker was transformed into an
object to be motivated and manipulated.

By the late 1920s and early 1930s, a new branch of the profession appeared under the heading of "personnel management," replete with studies of industrial psychology. Researchers like F. J. Roethlisberger and Elton Mayo instructed managers in increasing employee productivity. Here again, managers were to be the "thinkers" and workers were to be the "doers." This concept of "white collar" versus "blue collar" continues to exist in today's management as it follows the traditional hierarchical pattern of management.

Following World War II, professional management came into its own. No longer did it seem advantageous to promote from the shop floor; universities now had production lines turning out MBAs to whet the appetite of industry for professional managers. This bringing in of "outsiders" tended to exacerbate the alienation already being felt by the workers and helped to widen the gap between the blue-collar workers and management's understanding of their life on the production line.

During this period, behavioral scientists turned their attention to business organizations. Their concern was in seeking change in the basic climate of business organizations by creating open and free-flowing communication, increased productivity through concerted group effort, participative decision making, improved superior-subordinate relationships, integration and improvement of human and economic objectives, and enriched job content and individual freedom as motivation factors. This approach differed from the "human relations" movement which represented an attempt to break down formal and arbitrary boundaries of a bureaucratic organizational structure by being "friendly" toward their subordinates and trying to create a "big happy family." This movement was widely criticized for being manipulative and insincere and for ignoring the reality of productivity.

Such names as Douglas McGregor, Frederick Herzberg, Rensis Likert, Chris Argyris, Abraham Maslow, Robert Blake, and Jane Mouton come to mind when considering the influence of behavioral science upon industry. All of the above have made unique contributions to the growing body of knowledge of how and why people behave as they do in the work setting.

THE PRESENT STATUS OF MANAGEMENT

What has gone wrong in the field of management? After World War II, Britain sent businessmen to America to learn the secrets of the spectacular success of U.S. industry. Japan eagerly adopted the know-how of U.S. business methods as an entry into the postwar industrial world.

That era of prosperity and productivity no longer exists. Today U.S. industry is plagued by chronic absenteeism and work stoppages. The average number of days per year lost to industrial disputes for every 1,000 employees is 1,349 in the United States and 788 in Britain, compared to 39 in Sweden, 244 in Japan, and 56 in West Germany. U.S. productivity is not keeping pace with other countries. Therefore, it is not surprising that the Japanese can make a car and ship it here for $1,500 less than it costs a U.S. automaker to produce and sell a comparable vehicle.

Low productivity is the gravest problem facing companies today. It is estimated that employees in the United States average only 5½ productive hours in an 8-hour day. If this figure were increased only one half hour, it would boost the level by 10%. We have already seen in chapter 1 that the steady decline in productivity clearly shows the need for action by American industry to get back on the right track.

A TROUBLED MANAGEMENT

A wave of criticism, some of it valid, is being leveled at management from different directions. Dr. W. E. Deming, whose lectures helped launch quality control in Japan 30 years ago stated: "Managers blame their troubles on the work force whereas it is the fault of managers because the managerial systems are the problems."

Robert B. Reich, director of policy planning, Federal Trade Commission, felt that professional managers with their "management thinks—workers do" philosophy are at fault. He stated: "The symbols in which he (the professional manager) thinks and works are those of finance, law, accounting, and psychology. . . . Without any abiding commitment to the company, he is a master of the *quick fix*, yielding the sort of short-term profits institutional investors love. . . . The ideal of professional management has little to do with the messy and unpredictable tasks of producing real goods or services or working with real people."

Lewis H. Young, editor-in-chief of *Business Week*, offered criticism but also offered constructive advice when he stated:

> The question for American business is how to get those productivity increases without shutting down all of our plants. One way is to give workers some say in how they do their jobs. Quite often the man on the line knows the details of the job better than anyone else. Another way is to give supervisors and middle-level managers more autonomy. Almost every chief executive I meet talks of his frustrating failure to build a spirit of entrepreneurship in his company. As long as only the CEO can make decisions, nobody can be an entrepreneur. It is this kind of centralized control that is stifling creativity in corporations and turning U.S. companies into me-too producers who have to follow where the Japanese or Germans lead.

MANAGEMENT AND THE HUMAN DIMENSION

The present system with its built-in conflicts encouraged the perception that "head work" was the responsibility of managers only. As Alfred S. Warren, Jr., industrial relations vice-president of General Motors Corporation commented: "We're still living in the 1930's world, paying for the use of a worker's hands and not what he can offer mentally." In a similar vein, Michael Sonduck, corporate manager of work improvement at Digital Equipment Corporation, said: "One of the most dehumanizing assumptions ever made is that workers work and managers think. When we give shop-floor workers control over their work, they are enormously thoughtful."

From examining Japanese production systems, it is evident that quality is not something slapped on by inspecting the final product; it must be built in. To this end, executives in more and more American companies are scrutinizing the organizational device widely used by the Japanese for several decades—quality circles. Circles involve workers more intimately in the design of their own labors. They bring workers into better communication with one another and management. The results can be synergistic, with the participation leading to better understanding, individual development, greater self-respect, and stronger commitment to producing good results.

Quality circles as a process of management can be a means of changing the authoritarian style of traditional management to a participative management approach. The QC process will help break down the artificial wall between workers and management and render the workplace truly collaborative. Reich stated it in prophetic terms: "This will happen over the next decade because we have no choice but to make it happen if we are to sustain our economic base. . . . Our workplaces will become more equitable, secure and democratic . . . because international competition will require that they be so."

Job Design and Quality Circles

Job design, the techniques by which a job is developed or enlarged, in its current sense, is the specification of job content, method, and relationships in order to satisfy technological and organizational requirements, as well as the social and personal requirements of the jobholder. This approach that encompasses human needs for meaningful and self-fulfilling work, as well as technology, has its roots in the behavioral sciences. Jobs are being designed to "fit the job to the man" in the hope that greater motivation will result. The underlying assumption is that motivation is integral to higher productivity, *since productivity is a function of efficient use of material and human resources.*

There are several approaches to job design, their relative value seemingly depending upon the firm's product or service requirements, its managerial style, and the motivational level of the work force. The principal approaches currently in use include:

- *Job rotation,* in which the employee moves from one task to a related task within his or her "home" work area.

- *Job enlargement,* in which several related tasks are assumed by an employee who previously performed a single task or handled a fractionalized part of an operation.

- *Job enrichment,* in which the difficulty of the basic task is increased to demand more of the employee's capabilities, and in which the employee accepts more responsibility and accountability for "managing" the job.

- *Plan-Do-Control,* in which the job is enriched by the employee's adding the "managerial" function of planning and controlling to the actual doing of the job.

- *Work simplification,* in which the job is examined and analyzed by steps to eliminate unnecessary or duplicated tasks, combine logical sequences into a single job, and improve methods of doing the job.

The manager who wants to improve the job-employee match or remove some of the boredom from work is faced with two contradictory approaches. On the one hand, traditional "scientific management" and the industrial engineer call for the programming and standardization of specialized tasks using the techniques of work simplification, methods design, process and activity charts, and so on. On the other hand, the behavioral scientists tell us that task specialization is bad and that we should engineer the job so that employees want to channel their interests toward their work.

These two approaches have tended to exaggerate differences rather than similarities, and a natural schism has developed. The route to overcoming the apparent contradiction between "scientific management" and "behavioral science" lies in a marriage of the two. This third or *integrated* approach is one that is based on *job development* and that fits the pattern manifested by quality circles. Table 5-1 shows these three approaches to job development. Note that the concept and the practice of quality circles integrate almost everything we know about work and the human dimension of behavioral science.

Job Development and Job Design*

At the outset, it is useful to distinguish between *job development* and *job satisfaction*. Many people assume that job development is confined to improved working conditions, fringe benefits, and other "hygiene" factors associated with "job satisfaction." This, of course, is not the case. Job development means more—it means self-

---

*The term "job development" is similar to, but more comprehensive than, the popular terms "job enlargement" or "job enrichment." It is unfortunate that the latter two terms have become associated with gimmickry such as horizontal loading of jobs, focus on salary aspects, and failure to deliver on motivational promises. Job development, on the other hand, focuses on all three areas of worker utilization: the job, the employee, and the team or work group of which the employee is a part. See William N. Penzer, *Productivity and Motivation Through Job Engineering* (New York: AMACOM, 1973).

TABLE 5-1
Comparison of Three Different Approaches to Job Development

Scientific Management	Behavioral Science	Integrated (with Quality Circles)
Specialization of tasks	Provide task variety to avoid boredom	Be allowed to monitor their own work pace
Minimize number of operations one employee performs	Enlarge the job to meet the skills and ability of the worker	Be allowed to determine which methods are best for accomplishing a particular task
Eliminate unnecessary motions and operations	Provide feedback on performance	Be assigned primary responsibility for quality
No idle or waiting time	Provide job closure or job identification	Be encouraged to be the true job experts
Let the worker work and the supervisor plan and control	Self-control of significant aspects of the work	Be encouraged to become involved in decision making regarding unit problems and solutions
	Participation in problem solving, planning, and controlling	Be provided opportunity for more responsible, challenging, and self-fulfilling work assignments
	Opportunity to learn new skills	

actualizing work. Job design is the use of techniques by which a job is developed.

Perhaps the best-known example of "job satisfaction" and quality of worklife involves Volvo, the giant Swedish automobile manufacturer. An entire plant was built to make the jobs of the workers more satisfying. Assembly lines were avoided wherever possible, and each employee could do a variety of tasks. Working conditions were designed to be the most pleasing of any auto plant in the world. But all this did nothing for productivity, despite the fact that employees were significantly more satisfied. The management of Volvo found out at great cost that increasing *job satisfaction* does not result in rising productivity.

Walter A. Fallon, board chairman of Eastman Kodak Company, gives one of the company's rules for productivity: "Realize that people enjoy working productively because they experience satisfaction through self-improvement. People like the sense of accomplishment that comes from doing a good job even better." This is job satisfaction *through* job development.

It has been estimated that substantially more than half of the jobs in both the private and public sectors, in both manufacturing and service industries, require little more skill than driving an automobile. There is no way to validate this estimate, but it does give us an indication of the potential for productivity increases if this reservoir of talent were put to work. A major possibility for achieving this potential is the use of *job development.*

Prudential Insurance Company has what is perhaps the largest job development and redesign program in the world, affecting hundreds of jobs and involving several thousand people. The reason given for undertaking such a project was the prediction that the company would find it more and more difficult to find people to perform "dumb" jobs. It therefore became desirable to change the nature of jobs —to enrich, expand, and develop them.

Principles of Job Development

There are three fundamental principles of job development:

1. Vertical loading
2. Closure
3. Feedback

Notice that the application of each principle depends upon the establishment of targets or standards or *measures of productivity improvement objectives (results)*.

VERTICAL LOADING

Vertical loading refers to the job-employee match previously described wherein the employee's job responsibility and decision-making participation is enlarged to meet the individual's skills, abilities, and potential. This is in contrast to the "ratchet principle" or traditional *horizontal* loading, which merely increases the volume of work that an employee does at a particular level of difficulty. For example, the restaurant busboy who is assigned the additional duties of sweeping up the floor is experiencing horizontal loading without additional responsibility or discretion. However, if he is given responsibility for inventory control of dishes and tableware, he is experiencing vertical job loading. It becomes immediately apparent that *the delegation of the manager's own duties is the best way to enlarge the jobs of subordinates.*

At Citibank in New York, the entire production force of over 3,000 employees is being converted from functional (e.g., filing, editing, statements) work to a work-design format. Now each employee, instead of working at a somewhat boring task of limited scope, has his or her cathode ray tube (CRT) to handle all the account work, which includes research, processing, checking, and scheduling.

In one plant at Nabisco, Inc., a cookie line that was organized in assembly-line fashion was vertically integrated. Now one supervisor is in charge of the entire line, from flour mixing through baking and packaging.

CLOSURE

Closure is the characteristic of a job that provides the employees with a sense of contributing to the organization and of identifying with the end product of their work. The typical assembly-line job fails to provide closure because the workers perform miniscule, repetitive parts of the whole job, and begin to get the feeling that they are "nameless, faceless cogs in the big machine."

In the case of the busboy mentioned above, closure could be provided if his job were assigned the responsibility for the purchase of supplies within a given budget. The budget is the measure or the productivity objective (result).

Many traditional managers think that when people punch a time clock they know they are working because being physically present means the same as working. This isn't necessarily so. Many workers perform their jobs while they are mentally a thousand miles away. What is happening is that the autocratic supervisor and the bureaucratic organization have suppressed the natural desire of the individual to feel that he or she is making a contribution. People contribute when they feel that they have a hand in shaping the final result.

At International Harvester's plant in Gulfport, Mississippi, instead of using the traditional assembly-line methods, work teams are assigned to equip tractors with front-end loaders, backhoes, and other components. Workers and managers believe that this method promotes identification with the finished product and the customer.

R. B. Barry Corporation, manufacturer of women's slippers, had a plant in Goldsboro, North Carolina that was organized according to modern assembly-line methods and industrial engineering techniques. The company scrapped the system and went to a more elementary mechanical team approach in which work teams handled the complete task. They also learned other operations and rotated jobs. They received same-day feedback on output and quality. Productivity went up 50%.

FEEDBACK

The responsible worker, one who participates in setting his or her individual or team *productivity objectives* (results expected), requires information for *self-control* — performance against the target, standard, or measure. Such feedback must be timely, relevant to performance, and operational—not historical information from a variance report from the accounting department or the data-processing center. Obviously, information for self-control can only be relevant if it relates to a target or measure.

Feedback on performance is a necessary part of job development, and it makes good supervisory sense. Too frequently superiors depend upon variance reports or annual performance appraisals to provide feedback. These formal devices are not only too infrequent but in almost every case are too late to provide the type of "real-time" feedback required.

The notion of real-time feedback can be understood by using an analogy. A bowler ordinarily rolls the ball and gets immediate feedback on the number of pins he had knocked down. Now imagine that a curtain is thrown up immediately after the ball is rolled so that the bowler is unable to see how many pins he had knocked down. Somewhat in the manner of an employee, he shouts: "How did I do?" and somewhat in the manner of the manager, someone shouts from behind the curtain: "Don't worry, I will let you know [by variance report] next week." Obviously, no one would want to bowl under these circumstances because no feedback on performance is available.

The message here is that the supervisor should provide this feedback or, better still, build it into the job. Feedback is also a necessary ingredient of self-development, coaching, and counseling.

For many years, Emery Air Freight conducted unsuccessful industrial engineering studies to determine the optimum number of calls for a truck driver. Yet drivers, with little or no analysis, could nearly always control their own schedule and raise the number of calls significantly once they knew how many calls they had actually made as compared to the numbers they had planned to make.

Work Teams and Job Development: Implications for Quality Circles

The principles of job development are equally applicable to individual workers and work teams. Indeed, the team approach provides the best of both worlds: job development *plus* the advantages of the productivity improvement teams outlined earlier in this chapter.

It is not necessary that teams be comprised of employees with the same or similar functional work skills. Multiskilled teams can be equally effective.

Summary: Quality Circles and the Human Dimension

A study by the American Management Association concluded that the 1980s in all probability "will become the decade of the employee." The AMA study said that while it is no longer true that a company is the lengthened shadow of a single individual, top management does establish the tone and style. Top management will have to lead "in a climate of openness, trust and participation in which the self-motivation of every single member of the organization is encouraged."

In this chapter, we have attempted to integrate the concepts of productivity improvement, motivation, and the need for a new management style. None of these is in opposition to the others. All are interactive and together comprise the *people* dimension of productivity. If a firm organizes a quality circle effort, it will inevitably improve productivity. If it organizes a productivity effort, it must be sensitive to the quality circle concept. And an understanding of the concepts and the principles of motivation is essential to both.

Taken together, productivity, motivation, and quality circles represent change in an organization. Change cannot be achieved by dictum; it cannot be nurtured by lip service. Productivity should be accepted for what it is—*a way of managerial life*.

6

An Appraisal: Are You Ready for Productivity and Quality Circles?

ap-praise: to give an expert judgment of
the value of merit of
fea-si-ble: capable of being used or dealt
with successfully

WEBSTER'S DICTIONARY

The two movements of productivity improvement and quality circles are accelerating in response to the urgency for increased output on the one hand and for quality of work life and job satisfaction on the other. Despite the obvious complementary nature of the two movements, they have not been united into a single approach that meets both the need for productivity and the need for job satisfaction. The primary vehicle to facilitate such an approach is a productivity improvement program (PIP), and an essential component of such a program is quality circles.

Popular interest in the QC movement is somewhat analogous to a Boeing 747 that is coming toward you on the horizon. At first it seems to be hardly moving. As it comes closer, both the size and the speed accelerate rapidly until the plane seems to be zooming in at you. The speed and the size were the same all along; it is your awareness that changes because it is now upon you. So it is with the QC "movement." We are becoming more aware of this movement, but our lead time for doing something about it is growing shorter.

In this chapter we argue that quality circles are really a subset of a larger concept that we can label *productivity improvement*. If circles are to achieve their potential, they should be operated as part of a larger *productivity improvement program* (PIP).* To implement QCs as a separate or independent program is to risk inattention from and lack of acceptability to both managers and employees alike. We have witnessed the coming and going of various management "movements." Zero defects, value analysis, management by objectives (MBO),

* For a complete action plan and a description of a productivity improvement program, see Joel Ross, *People, Profits, and Productivity* (Englewood Cliffs: Prentice-Hall, 1981).

cost-benefit analysis, sensitivity training, organization development—the list goes on. Frequently, managers and employees pay lip service to such "movements" but make no real commitment. Or a technique may not be used to its full potential because of lack of attention or because it is perceived as a *management* program. Quality circles face the danger of meeting a similar fate because they can easily be perceived by workers as management's attempt to blame them, the workers, for lack of quality or production.

A *productivity improvement program*, then, means taking an organizational approach that will achieve these objectives:

1. *Utilize human resources through the vehicle of quality circles.*
2. *Bridge the gap between quality circles and higher levels of managers.*
3. *Integrate employees into a total organization effort to improve productivity.*
4. *Gain wider acceptance and recognition of quality circles and the contribution they can make.*

If achieved, these objectives lead to greater synergism in the company. Workers are involved in the design of their own labors and are brought into better communication with one another and with management. Their participation leads to better understanding, individual development, greater respect, and a commitment to achieving better results.

Circles can be effective only if they are implemented properly. The purpose of appraisal, then, is to evaluate your readiness for:

A productivity improvement program

and

quality circles

Appraising Your Readiness for Productivity Improvement

The first step in undertaking a productivity improvement program is to conduct an appraisal of where you are, where you want to go, and how you plan to get there. The objective is to identify opportunities and problems within the organizational environment and to lay the groundwork for action planning to follow. It could be termed "strategic productivity planning." More specifically, the appraisal process surveys and evaluates both *operating* and *management* systems for the purpose of identifying the potential for improving productivity and implementing a program.

IS YOUR COMPANY READY FOR PRODUCTIVITY?

Two questions arise: "Are you sure you want to increase productivity?" and "Are you ready to start a program?"

Managers will frequently reply "yes" to the first question without realizing what is involved. They pay lip service to the notion but are unwilling to spend the necessary time. They believe that productivity involves a package of techniques that can easily be put in place. This, of course, is not the case. *Productivity means change*. New methods and systems may be required, an appraisal of current practices is needed, and, most of all, a reorientation of beliefs about relationships with people may be necessary. The major dimension is the human-resource environment and philosophy—the values held by top management.

Regarding the second question—Are you ready to start a program?—a certain managerial environment should exist, or be established, before the chances of success can be estimated as good. The American Productivity Center in Houston, Texas, lists eight thought-provoking questions that should be answered as an indication of whether or not you need preliminary groundwork to ensure that your program has the best chance of being successful. These are:

- Are management/employee/union relations in the company such that these parties would not view negatively an expressed desire to tackle head-on the pressing issue of productivity improvement?

  Comment: Confidence is needed for everyone to give the program a try.

- Does the company have a positive rating on working conditions, pay levels, company personnel policy and administration, and job security?

  Comment: If these ingredients are out of line, the climate might not be right to begin.

- Is top management willing to share with employees at all levels the economic benefits that can be derived from improvements in productivity?

  Comment: Unwillingness to share benefits reduces credibility and increases the feeling in employees of being exploited.

- Is the company's accounting system "healthy" and flexible enough to accept changes required to effectively portray productivity data?

  Comment: Some integration between productivity measurement and the accounting system may be desirable.

- Is top management willing to listen to the employees?

  Comment: Impetus for the program comes from the top down, but most improvement ideas will come from the bottom up.

- Is the technology employed by the company flexible so that improvements in the organization of work can be made?

  Comment: Inflexible technology or production systems may reduce the potential for productivity improvement.

- Does top management believe that the company's performance depends substantially on the efforts of its human resources?

  Comment: Only people can get you increased productivity.

- Is the company serious about improving its economic performance?

  Comment: If the company is content with its progress or if "managerial menopause" has set in, forget it.

IDENTIFYING PROBLEMS AND OPPORTUNITIES*

The approach to an organization productivity appraisal is not too different from that involved in a traditional management audit. This is to be expected, because productivity improvement is really a function of how well the management process is performed.

The objective for appraisal is to *survey* and *evaluate* both operating and management systems in order to identify areas, techniques, and plans for improvement.

The Survey Phase. In the *survey* phase of an appraisal, the systems are reviewed to identify existing practices in order to later seek out unproductive or improper methods. The hundreds of items that could be surveyed depend upon the nature of the organization and the scope of the appraisal. Some factors that might cause trouble are shown in Table 6-1. Although the factors listed there were developed for a research and development organization, the same list would be appropriate for any type of company or operation.

---

* A more detailed approach to appraisal has been prepared by the American Productivity Center in Houston. That organization has prepared a comprehensive manual for this purpose.

TABLE 6-1
Twenty-five Factors Most Likely To Cause Serious Counterproductivity Within R&D Organizations

1. Ineffective planning, direction, and control
2. Overinflated organization structures
3. Overstaffing
4. Insufficient management attention to productivity, and to the identification and elimination of counterproductive factors within the organization
5. Poor internal communication
6. Inadequate technology exchange
7. Insufficient or ineffective investment in independent research and development (IR&D) efforts
8. Poor psychological work environment
9. Lack of people orientation in management—insufficient attention to employee motivation
10. Poor employment practices
11. Ineffective structuring of assignments
12. Lack of effective performance appraisal and feedback
13. Insufficient attention to low producers
14. Technological obsolescence
15. Ineffective reward systems which inadequately correlate individual productivity and compensation.
16. Lack of equitable parallel managerial and technical promotion ladders
17. Lack of equity in operations
18. Ineffective customer interface
19. Ineffective engineering/production interface
20. Ineffective subcontractor/supplier interface and control
21. Operational overcomplexity—constrictive procedures and red tape.
22. Excessive organizational politics and gamesmanship
23. Excessive provincialism
24. Ineffective management development
25. Inadequate investment in and lack of proper maintenance of capital facilities

Source: Hughes Aircraft Company, R&D Productivity, 1978

118

The range of *operating systems* that might be included in the survey are as follows:

Operating Systems	Support Systems	Administrative Systems
Sales	Personnel	General Accounting
Manufacturing	Design	Data Processing
Purchasing	Quality Control	Production Control
Shipping	Maintenance	Marketing Services
Warehousing	Plant Engineering	Inventory Control
Etc.	Etc.	Etc.

Management systems might include an inventory of good and bad management practices and productivity improvement techniques in the following illustrative areas:

Planning	Organization	Control
Strategic planning (including major objectives and policies)	Structure, responsibility, and resources	Accounting system and reports
	Human-resource organization and records	Productivity measures
The planning system (developmental, operational, financial, functional, etc.)	Extra layers of organization and overlapping duties	Performance measurement analysis
Etc.	Management values	Project and program control
	Employee relations climate	Etc.
	Productivity incentives	
	Training and development	
	Etc.	

As a part of the survey phase, the appraisal might include an *attitude survey*. Since productivity is the result of people's behavior and this behavior is largely a result of attitudes, the best way to change behavior is to change attitudes. This cannot be done unless existing attitudes are determined. Opinion and supposition are not dependable means for making this determination. We tend to perceive attitudes as we would like them to be or to present glowing reports because to do otherwise might reflect on our competency. Surveys also represent a report card for management that tells it how well or poorly it is doing its job in the employees' eyes.

Evaluation Phase. The *evaluation* phase of a production appraisal program attempts to evaluate the unproductive methods and techniques and the performance of units, departments, and individuals for the purpose of identifying opportunities for improvement. Wherever possible, productivity measures should be used for that purpose. These measures may be macro (company-wide) or micro (functional or departmental).

The evaluation will provide the basis upon which company, unit, and departmental action plans will subsequently be developed. It will also provide the vehicle for participation, communication, and implementation.

As stated earlier, managing a productivity improvement program is no different than managing any other program, function, or activity. It requires that *objectives* be set, *plans* developed, *organization* structured, and progress *controlled*. However, the management of productivity cannot be applied like a Band-Aid over an existing management system that has serious shortcomings. If good plans and controls do not exist within the framework of a good organizational structure, and if all the other manifestations of good organization and management are not present, then a productivity improvement system becomes a crutch to overcome bad practice.

With good management systems, we can *plan, organize,* and *control* a productivity improvement program.

FACTORS OF PRODUCTIVITY SUCCESS

In a 1981 research study of companies with successful productivity programs, the Kearney consulting organization asked two questions of company executives:

1. How do you know a productivity program is needed? and, after it is installed:
2. How do you know if it is still effective?

Patterns of general similarity emerged and are grouped in Table 6-2 into three broad factor areas and then cast into a checklist for self appraisal. The research suggests that companies with leading programs can answer these questions and the top 5% of companies can answer most questions positively.

TABLE 6-2
A Checklist of Self-Appraisal Questions for Productivity Improvement*

General Business Factors

---

1. Are *profits and return on investment* (ROI) percentages in the upper quartile of the industry? (Near-term Results)
2. Would the past five-year *trend* of profit and ROI performance, if continued for the next three years, place or sustain the company in the upper quartile of its industry? (Long-term Results)
3. Are profit and ROI percentage *results in "down years"* better than industry averages? (Spot Results)
4. Are *assets deployed* effectively (is it time to divest or promote select businesses) in light of current strategic direction? (Product)
5. Are gains from new customers *offsetting the business* from lost customers? (Quality, Service, Image)

Table 6-2 (continued)

Resource Utilization Factors

1. Is the percentage of sales growth greater than percent growth in *interest expense?* (Money)
2. Are trends of *asset utilization* outperforming industry trends? (Assets)
   — Inventory turnover
   — Sales/fixed asset replacement value
3. Are *general and administrative* (G&A) results and trends in the upper quartile of the industry? (People and Technology)
   — Exempt count/total G&A count
   — Exempt salary/total G&A salaries
     (Management Utilization)
4. Are most key promotions from within? Is the percentage of sales growth greater than the percentage of recruiting costs growth? (People and Technology)
5. Are at least 20% of *reports*, forms, and routine analyses dropped or reduced in frequency each year? (Information)
   — G&A count/investment in mechanization
   — Profit growth/systems investment growth

Productivity Program Factors

1. Is the productivity program *effective and efficient?*
   — Profit growth/count of project personnel
   — Profit growth/program cost growth
2. Does the program have broad *scope?*
   — Corporate, division, and plant
   — Indirect, clerical, knowledge worker, and management
   — Assets, capital, technology, and information
3. Are the right *approaches and techniques* employed for the business situation?
   — Profit crisis
   — Harvest, middle performer
   — Leading performer
   — Opportunistic

4. Are all the *fundamental success factors* employed?
   — Involvement/commitment
     • Management committee hierarchy agenda
     • Built-in productivity goals
     • Dedication of key people
   — Broad perspective
     • Scope of productivity
     • "ABC" of projects aimed at near and long term results
   — Work on the right things
     • "A" project plan and review
     • Project management controls
   — Know where going and if getting there
     • Periodic business appraisal
     • Documented mission, goals
     • Results oriented measurement
   — Singularity of responsibility
     • Nonduplicated or compensating assignment for outputs and resources
     • Standards of performance
     • Management productivity measures

Adapted by permission from A. T. Kearney, Inc., Management Consultants, Managing For Excellence: A Research Study on the State-Of-The-Art of Productivity Programs in the United States, Chicago, 1981.

Appraising the Feasibility of Quality Circles

Many of the earlier questions in this chapter related to appraising your readiness for a *productivity improvement program* (PIP) also apply to implementing quality circles. Indeed, as we stated earlier, it may not be wise to implement quality circles without first considering the larger issue of a productivity improvement program. Stated another way, if you get a passing grade on your appraisal for a productivity improvement program, you are well on the way to success in a quality circle program.

It only remains to consider a few appraisal questions that are peculiar to the QC effort. These questions are summarized below.

Question	Yes	No
1. Should I begin with a pilot circle?	( )	( )
Or should I implement the program company-wide?	( )	( )
Comment: It is generally wise to start in a small way with a pilot project. This approach can demonstrate that circles do work and can serve as a testing ground for the operation of an expanded effort.		
2. Should the objective(s) be related primarily to the "people dimension" (i.e., personal and team development)?	( )	( )
Or should the objective(s) be related to tangible and quantitative results having to do with quality and productivity?	( )	( )
Comment: Either, or both, of these objectives are suitable. Whatever objective(s) is (are) adopted, a clear statement is necessary to avoid misperception and possible resentment from circle members.		
3. Do I have the support of:		
a. Upper Management?	( )	( )
Comment: If the management style is theory X or autocratic, circles are unlikely to work unless a change is achieved or a more participative style adopted.		
b. Middle Management? Production Supervision?	( )	( )
Comment: Line managers at this level have a variety of feelings, usually negative, about circles. Essentially they fear an encroachment on their authority and		

Question	Yes	No

fail to see any direct reward for themselves.

Many production supervisors have a work history that is centered on a boss-subordinate relationship with workers. They see this role as being compromised by circles. Part of this reluctance to accept circles can be overcome by carefully explaining the concept and the role of circles. Remaining skepticism is often reduced after experience and success with the QC effort.

4. Is the economic climate right?   ( )   ( )

Comment: Circle members cannot be expected to develop cost- or personnel-saving ideas if it means the possible loss of jobs for themselves or their friends. Nor is a frequently changing employment level conducive to acceptance. Turnover among members reduces the chance of building a team. It is therefore better to begin the circle effort when economic conditions are relatively stable.

5. Has an attitude survey been conducted?   ( )   ( )

Comment: It is clearly not appropriate to adopt circles on a superficial basis or in the face of significant opposition. A carefully conducted survey among personnel will provide a better prediction of success or failure. This survey should be done following an in-depth orientation session.

6. Do I have the resources?   ( )   ( )

Comments: People and funds are required. Circles require an in-house coordinator, a facilitator, and a leader for each circle. These should be your "least

Question	Yes	No

affordable" people and they should be re-
spected by workers and have a humanis-
tic orientation. All personnel receive
their regular pay for attendance at
meetings or other circle activities. In addition, a consultant (if used), and incentives (if awarded) are required.

7. Do I have a sponsor for the pilot pro-
gram?   ( )   ( )

Comment: If it is decided to begin with a
pilot project (this is recommended)
rather than an across-the-board approach, it is important to identify and
gain acceptance from a high potential
(HYPO) department or location. The cri-
teria for such a department or location
are: (a) it should be headed by a manager
who has both the authority and desire to
implement one or more circles, (b) it
should have a high potential for improvement and a desire for improvement, (c) it should have a measurable
output and yardsticks of quality and productivity, (d) it should be a "homoge-
neous" location, i.e., one that is similar to
a wide range of other locations so that
results are perceived as applicable elsewhere. This will avoid the "Yes, but
we're different" syndrome.

Unions: A Special Case

There is little doubt that quality circles and quality of
work life (QWL) programs—a movement of which circles
are a subset—are increasing in American industry and
gaining acceptance among union members and leaders.

It is generally recognized that workers want more from the job than traditional union benefits. This has been summarized by Lloyd McBride, president of the United Steel Workers, as follows:

> Basic to the solution of productivity is the involvement of the worker in the decision making process. Industry must accept the fact that workers are quite often aware of problems and solutions that would be helpful to the boss if they were included in the process.

Labor unions today face a paradox. On the one hand, they tend to frown on many elements of QWL programs because of the traditional fears that productivity means speedup, job security will be threatened, standards of performance will be tightened, and QWL is a union-busting activity. On the other hand, union management is beginning to realize that members are no longer content with the traditional union benefits.

The attitude of many unions has begun to soften toward QWL programs. Today the United Auto Workers offers general support for the programs. Experience at several auto plants indicates that QWL programs have dramatically improved relations between worker and manager and reduced chances of local strikes. Other unions that have endorsed such programs include the Bakery & Confectionery Workers, the Newspaper Guild, the American Federation of State, County, and Municipal Employees, and the United Food & Commercial Workers. The Communication Workers of America are in the developmental stage of endorsing QWL methods.

In 1980, the bargaining pact in the steel industry became a landmark event in labor negotiations. The settlement moved labor relations away from the traditional adversary confrontation between workers and bosses toward a more cooperative approach to common problems in the workplace. The United Steel Workers (USW) and the com-

panies agreed to set up "labor-management participation teams" in an effort to make jobs more meaningful for workers and more productive for the companies. The problem-solving teams discuss such items as production efficiency, product quality, safety and health, employee morale, and absenteeism, as well as how supervisors deal with workers. This was the first union-management agreement adopted on an industrywide basis to deal with work-improvement ideas to relieve worker alienation and to speed up lagging productivity.

It is unlikely that a QWL program can be successful in a unionized organization without union involvement. Both management and the union should avoid the traditional adversary relationship and cooperate in a program that will benefit everyone. A beginning can be found in establishing a *labor–management QWL and productivity committee.*

At a New York plant of one automaker, the situation was desperate. Operating costs were skyrocketing, and the plant was at the bottom of the company's system in quality, production, and efficiency. Labor-management relations were polarized into a climate of entrenched conflict.

Then everything changed. During a meeting to review a production reorganization, the usual management groups were present: industrial engineers, plant engineers, staff planners, and so on. Someone raised a simple point that had never been asked before: "Maybe we should ask the people who are actually going to be directly involved. They probably know a lot more about it that will help us too." This led ultimately to the involvement of workers on the line and eventually to "rap sessions," expanded involvement, and a joint union-management committee to oversee quality of work life in the plant. There have also been joint labor-management problem-solving committees. Out of this union-management cooperation has come spectac-

ular results. Grievances have been reduced by 98%, absenteeism by 36%, and selected production problems have been reduced by from 50% to 95%.

GETTING UNION ACCEPTANCE AND COOPERATION

It is evident that quality circles will fail if the classic adversary relationship between management and the union prevails. In order to avoid this relationship and get acceptance, if not enthusiasm, these actions will help:

1. *Be upfront.* Involve the union in the early stages and maintain a climate of honesty and trust. Do not "paper over" the conditions surrounding QC implementation and be straightforward about objectives and policies.

2. *Quality circle concerns are not union concerns.* Make it clear that circles are not a threat to the unions. Traditional concerns of the union such as pay, benefits, and working conditions are not the subjects of QC discussions.

3. *Jobs are not threatened.* No one will lose a job or be laid off as a direct result of QC recommendation or improvement in quality or productivity.

4. *Maintain union participation and support.*

7

Getting Organized for Quality Circles

In factory after factory in Japan everyone inside is trying to whip us. If we don't get that attitude we literally won't survive.

WILLIAM A. COATES, Executive Vice President, Westinghouse

The above comment by Westinghouse executive William Coates reflects a growing realization by U.S. companies that the rigid American management style of the past is now out-of-date. A whole family of approaches to managing work is coming into prominence, and the most recognizable and popular device is the quality circle. Westinghouse is an example of one company that has wholeheartedly embraced the concept. As of mid-1981, the firm had more than 600 circles with more being added every day. *Fortune* magazine called it "Westinghouse's Cultural Revolution."

Quality circles are not an organization within themselves; rather, they are a system within the organizational hierarchy of the company. Achieving improved productivity through QCs is not just a matter for top management alone. It is an "all-hands" evolution and requires the participation of people at all levels. In order to achieve this participation, organizations need to make employees and managers aware of the importance of productivity and the need for involvement. As the president of Honeywell remarked, "You just don't put out a memo and say 'be participative you jerk.'"

Quality circles aren't just going to happen. They need to be *organized*. This implies a program structure, the assignment of tasks and responsibilities, and the involvement of people.

The normal organizational components involved in quality circles and their relationships, shown in figure 7-1, are:

- Top Management
- Steering Committee
- Coordinator

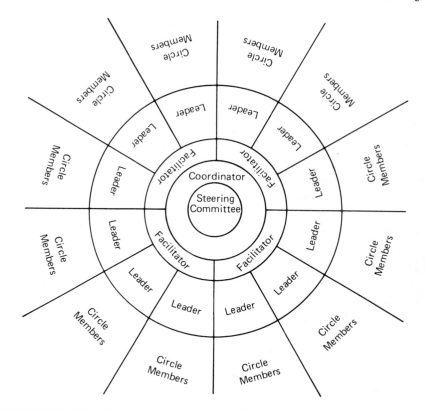

FIGURE 7-1. The Organization for Quality Circles

- Facilitator
- Circle Leaders
- Circles and Circle Members

Top Management

It cannot be repeated too frequently that top management support is essential for QC success. Without full and active support from the chief executive officer, the QC program will probably fail.

In addition to giving enthusiastic support to the circle program, and encouraging it as a way of organizational life, management can take these specific actions:

Be supportive by:

- Allowing circles to meet during normal working hours.
- Placing a high priority on circle meetings.
- Allowing cross-attendance between circles when working on joint projects.
- Providing adequate meeting areas, equipment, and supplies.
- Including circle activities as part of monthly reports and other activity reports.
- Authorizing selective attendance at outside conferences.
- Supporting circle activities in speeches, presentations, and public relations media.
- Including circle activities as a part of organizational goals.

Be participative by:

- Attending meetings.
- Following up on circle projects with time and money.
- Following up with leaders.
- Respecting the autonomy of circles.
- Encouraging management presentations as an essential part of activities.
- Implementing approved recommendations without delay.
- Responding quickly to circle recommendations. If impossible to comply, providing a detailed explanation.

Steering Committee

Composed of a cross section of line and staff top executives, the steering committee guides the implementation of the program after it determines major goals, policies, and procedures. It is the "board of directors" for the program. The committee establishes operational guidelines and controls the rate of expansion. Individual committee members may serve as a resource for solving problems in specific areas.

In addition to high-level management, the steering committee might include one or more representatives from middle management and the production area (e.g., production supervisors or foremen). Such participation not only lends applied points of view to deliberations but helps overcome the perception that circles are a "management" program. For these same reasons, some companies are including circle leaders as well as one or more production workers in the steering committee.

A typical statement of steering committee duties is shown in Figure 7-2.

FIGURE 7-2. The Steering Committee (Suggested by the International Association of Quality Circles).

Steering committee (the Quality Circle "Board of Directors") members are representatives of major organization components or functions. The following is a checklist of functions that should be performed by this group:

- Prepare objectives
- Prepare implementation plan to achieve objectives
- Identify milestones
- Determine funding arrangements
- Establish qualifications for facilitator
- Select facilitator
  —Determine who facilitator reports to
  —Determine office arrangements for facilitator

FIGURE 7-2. (Continued)

- Schedule familiarization presentations to wide variety of organizations
- Determine what circles can work on (e.g., quality, cost, safety, company policy, union personnel, design)
- Determine tie-in with suggestions program
- Establish baseline measurements
- Determine publicity approach
- Identify organizations for pilot program
- Decide how organization will learn about quality circles
  For example:
    Company newspaper
    Mass gathering in auditorium
    Letters to home
    Numerous small group sessions
    One-on-one
- Determine starting dates for pilot circles
- Identify leaders for pilot program
- Decide on frequency of circle meetings
- Meet regularly (minimum once monthly)
- Periodically review program milestones
- Identify individual or group to whom steering committee will make report
- Establish what rewards and recognition will be used (in addition to management presentations) For example:
    Quality circle newsletter
    Company newspaper
    Photos on bulletin boards
    Pins, plaques, certificates
    Copy of IAQC quality circle quarterly to leaders
    Cash awards
- Tie-in with the union

Coordinator

The coordinator supervises facilitators and maintains overall administration of the program. Depending on the company's size, a coordinator may not be required and that duty would then be performed by the facilitator. This situation would most likely occur in the smaller company without multi-divisions or plants.

The organizational *location* of the coordinator (or facilitator if he or she performs these duties) varies widely in practice. Although you might expect the coordination role to be undertaken by the quality control department, this is frequently not the case. Justification can be made for location in any one of several departments. The advantages and the disadvantages of each can be described in Table 7-1.

Facilitator

The facilitator is the individual responsible for coordinating and directing the QC activities within the organization of which he or she is a part. Each is a member of the steering committee and is selected by that committee. The primary functions of the facilitator are to:

- Interface between circles, staff organizations, and management.
- Maintain appropriate records and prepare reports.
- Execute steering committee policy.
- Train circle leaders.
- Audit, monitor, and evaluate the program.
- Communicate with unit, division, and profit center managers on productivity and quality questions.
- Act as consultant, researcher, and disseminator of ideas.
- Act as teacher and technical consultant.

TABLE 7-1
Advantages and Disadvantages of Various Locations
for Quality Circle Coordinators

Department	Advantage	Disadvantage
Quality Control	1. Many circle problems are quality related. 2. The problem solving techniques used by circles are basic to the operation of quality control.	1. The scope of problems considered by circles may be limited to those that are quality related. 2. Quality control is not a line department, and members may view this location as lack of line support.
Personnel/Employee Relations	1. Focus is more likely to be on the important motivational implications of circles. 2. This may be a good "temporary home" until usefulness of circles has been proven.	1. Productivity and quality objectives may become secondary. 2. Members may perceive this location as representing the lack of line support.
Line Department	1. It focuses attention on line-related problems and benefits such as quality, productivity, and safety. 2. Line support makes the circle more credible.	1. It requires that line personnel be convinced of circle benefits.

Viewed against the structure of the organization, the facilitator's relationship to a circle is complementary. If the facilitator is able to establish a circle that has its own technical expertise or has access to such expertise and also direct access to management when it arrives at a solution, then the facilitator is able to provide limited assistance while developing other circles.

An important function of the facilitator in working with the quality circle and its leader is that of *team-building*—a process aimed at improving the problem-solving ability of team members. We see the facilitator's role more as a "process" consultant rather than as an "expert." It is his or her responsibility to develop the process awareness by which the team can look at itself, its functions, its method of working together, and its goals for change. In order to accomplish this purpose, the facilitator and the group work toward:

- A better understanding by each team member of his or her role in the group.
- An understanding of the area of work responsibilities and the freedom to work within its limitations.
- Better communication among team members about issues that affect the group's efficiency.
- Awareness of implications and costs of changing work.
- Greater support among team members.
- Increased commitment to shared objectives.
- Shared leadership.

Once the circle has been trained in problem-solving techniques such as histograms, cause-and-effect diagrams, data-collecting techniques, etc., the important role of the facilitator becomes that of using *process interventions*. Centering around the ongoing work of the group as it takes part in problem solving, process interventions are aimed at improving the team's task goals as well as helping the group to become a more cohesive unit.

Some process interventions aimed at accomplishing the *group task* include the following:

1. Helping the group members clarify an issue into a problem statement.
2. Suggesting that summarizing a problem discussion helps the group move toward its goal.
3. Suggesting the proper tools or techniques that may help define the problem.
4. Getting the group to face action implications and to plan.
5. Observing that a decision was made without group consensus.

Other process interventions are aimed at *group maintenance* (activities that affect the group's welfare and solidarity.) A group's awareness of its own process precedes the ability to make wise choices about managing time. Such actions as functional conflict, expression of feelings as well as point of view, and confrontation and acceptance of interdependence are issues that the facilitator and the group will have to deal with during group interaction. Process interventions aimed at group maintenance include the following examples:

1. Encouraging members of the group to work toward consensus, with each member feeling free to express feelings about the decision.
2. Giving nonjudgmental feedback as to dysfunctional behavior which is blocking group progress.
3. Reinforcing positive group-building behavior such as summarizing, initiating, clarifying, etc.

If the group flounders or progress is slowed because of some interaction within the group, then the facilitator needs to intervene in order to get the session back "on track." An example is the case in which the group is having difficulty establishing a meeting agenda. The facilitator, in order to encourage a group decision, might intervene as follows: "Last session many of you were concerned that if we start our agenda and do not finish it, this is upsetting. It is then safer to do a topic that we will finish. This is a natural reaction. I wonder whether this is important, or should we be concerned with making the time worthwhile?" Similarly, when one or two group members attempt to "take over" as leaders through dominance or other means, the facilitator may intervene with, "Our feelings about power are blocking us from being able to share the leadership around the table. We must resolve feelings about power before leadership will be shared."

The facilitator in team-building should help the group solve its own problems by making it aware of its own group process and the way that this process affects the quality of the team's work. As one facilitator remarked: "My role is to work myself out of a job with one circle so that I can start with another circle."

If facilitators consciously strive to avoid creating a dependency on the facilitator and his or her office during the training and early stages of the relationship with the circle, then independent and self-sufficient circles can develop.

It is not enough that the facilitator work only with the circles; management needs to be kept current with the program's progress. The facilitator must develop effective communications with personnel at all levels. His or her primary responsibility for reporting is to the steering committee where schedules are discussed, modifications drawn up, and progress of the circles reported.

Leader

The circle leader has the key position in an individual circle. Success or failure is usually a function of how well he or she performs the leader's role. In practice, the supervisor is usually chosen as the leader of a circle which is within his or her work area, although there is no reason why nonsupervisory personnel cannot act as leaders.

Quality circle leaders provide leadership for the circles, teach circle members the techniques, and are responsible for the operation of their respective circles. The leader also assures proper communication with management through such means as minutes of meetings, activity reports, and management presentations.

What really makes a circle successful is its members learning to work together as a group on problem solving. Making this happen calls for unusual leadership skills on the leader's part. The characteristics and the skills usually sought in a leader are summarized below:

Characteristics	Leadership Skills
Positive in outlook	Resolving conflict
People-oriented	Ability to delegate
Credible	Maintaining morale
Good listener	Negotiating commitment
Growth potential	Developing subordinates
Creative and innovative	Encouraging participation in decisions

Circles and Circle Members

Circles direct their attention to problems and projects under their control. The scope of these problems and projects is usually defined by the steering committee. Within this broad constraint, they have the prerogative to accept or refuse problems or projects regardless of the source.

Other items related to circle operations are summarized in the following:

Item	Comment
Conduct of Meetings	• Assure that each member has an equal voice: one person, one vote.
	• Use the quality circles techniques described in the training manual.
	• Set up schedules for meetings with due consideration for company workload.
Participation	• Participation is purely voluntary. No one can be pressured to participate, but some companies encourage workers and supervisors to volunteer with the understanding that they can drop out at any time.
Scope of Circle Consideration	• *Includes:*
	1. Identification, analysis, and implementation of solutions to problems under their control.
	2. Conducting presentations to management regarding specific recommendations, accomplishments, and status.
	• *Excludes:* Matters outside the charter, such as: Benefits Personnel policies relating to discipline, employment, and termination Grievances and other matters covered by the labor contract Product design Sales and marketing policies Interpersonal conflicts
Circle Size	• The most workable size is considered to be 5 to 12 members. If the number of volunteers exceeds this number, additional circles may become necessary.

Item	Comment
Name of Circle	• Opinion is divided. The title "quality circle" is widely used; but many organizations think that this name implies a focus on quality whereas productivity, cost reduction, and other objectives are equally important. It may be wise to consider a name or a title that brings greater local identity to the circle. Some examples of names in use are Cost Cutters, Bottom Liners, The PITS (Productivity Improvement Team), The Ps & Qs (Productivity and Quality), VIPs (Volunteers Interested in Productivity), TOPs (Turned On to Productivity), PICs (Performance Improvement Circles), and PLUS (Productivity Leads Us to Success).
Meetings	• Meetings are normally held one hour per week during normal working hours. For assembly-line operators or other operation where members cannot be spared, meetings are held on overtime immediately before or after the shift and overtime wages are paid.
Objectives	• Typical objectives include: Reduce errors and enhance quality Inspire team building and more effective teamwork Promote job involvement Increase morale and motivation Create a problem-solving capability Improve company communications Develop harmonious relationships Advance safety awareness Increase quality and cost awareness Enhance organizational synergism Expand personal growth and development

8

Implementing Quality Circles: The Action Plan

As far as I'm concerned, it's the only way to operate the business —there isn't any other way in today's world.

F. JAMES McDONALD, President
General Motors

The comment by Mr. McDonald, which opens this chapter, fairly reflects the accelerating acceptance of quality circles in American industry. Many firms are adopting the concept, and others wonder what they can do to get on the bandwagon.

In many respects, the first seven chapters of this book are a prelude to developing an action plan for starting a company quality circle program. A suggested action plan is outlined in this chapter.

For those companies already involved in such a program, this plan will serve as a check-off list for further refinement and modification. For those companies deciding to begin a program, the plan will provide a road map of actions to be taken. In either case, the plan's content is not cast in bronze. It is and should be flexible so that it may be changed to meet the particular needs of the organization.

We remind you that each major milestone and action step is discussed elsewhere in related chapters of the book. You may wish to refer to the appropriate description as an aid in developing your own plan.

The Action Plan

MAJOR MILESTONES

1. Background Research
2. Appraisal
3. Acceptance
4. Organization
5. Measurement
6. Awareness
7. Pilot Circle Project
8. Training

	Start	*Complete*	*Assigned to*

1. Background Research

1.1 DEVELOP INFORMATION BASE
    1.11 Conduct literature search ____ ____ ____
    1.12 Check industry and asso- ____ ____ ____
         ciation sources
    1.13 Contact International ____ ____ ____
         Association of Quality
         Circles (IAQC)
1.2 FIND OUT WHAT OTHERS HAVE DONE
    1.21 Attend circle conference ____ ____ ____
         or seminar
    1.22 Visit active circle pro- ____ ____ ____
         grams in other com-
         panies
    1.23 Visit local chapters of ____ ____ ____
         American Society of
         Training Directors
         (ASTD), American So-
         ciety of Personnel
         Administrators (ASPA),
         International Associa-
         tion of Quality Circles
         (IAQC)

2. APPRAISAL

2.1 CHECK YOUR READINESS TO BEGIN
    2.11 Should quality circles be ____ ____ ____
         an integral part of a
         broader *productivity im-*
         provement program? Is
         this program in place?

	Start	*Complete*	*Assigned to*
2.12 Have objectives been established?	___	___	___

2.12 Have objectives been established?
    Utilize human resources?
    Bridge gap between QCs and higher management levels?
    Integrate employees into a total productivity effort?
    Gain acceptance of QCs

2.13 Are you sure you want to start a program? It mean changes in methods and a reorientation of beliefs about relationships with people.   ___   ___   ___

2.14 Are you ready to start?   ___   ___   ___
    Do you have:
    ( ) Good employee and union relations?
    ( ) Working environment?
    ( ) Willingness to share benefits?
    ( ) Willingness to listen to people?
    ( ) Seriousness about improving productivity?
    ( ) A belief that performance depends substantially on human resources?

2.2 CONDUCT SELF-APPRAISAL REGARDING PRODUCTIVITY (see Table 6-2)
    ( ) General business factors   ___   ___   ___
    ( ) Resource utilization factors   ___   ___   ___
    ( ) Productivity program factors   ___   ___   ___

Assigned

Start   Complete   to

2.3 CONDUCT SELF-APPRAISAL REGARDING QUALITY CIRCLES

2.31 Do you have the support   _____   _____   _____
of:
( ) Upper management
( ) Middle management
( ) Production supervision
( ) Employees
( ) Union

2.32 Is the economic climate   _____   _____   _____
right?

2.33 Do you need an attitude   _____   _____   _____
survey?

2.34 Are resources available?   _____   _____   _____

2.4 IDENTIFY PROBLEMS AND OPPORTUNITIES

2.41 Evaluate unproductive   _____   _____   _____
methods and techniques
and performance of units
for purpose of identifying
the opportunities for im-
provement

2.42 Evaluate past produc-   _____   _____   _____
tivity performance using
industry measures and
trends over time

---

3. Acceptance

3.1 IDENTIFY LEVELS OF MANAGEMENT

Top management   _____   _____   _____
Middle management
Plant manager
Production manager
Superintendent
First-line supervisors

	Start	Complete	Assigned to

3.2 PREPARE PRESENTATION

   3.21 Select topics

       Milestones in QC develop-
ment in Japan and U.S.

       Comments of manage-
ment and workers in-
volved in circles

       Theoretical basis and
benefits

       Mechanics of circle
operations

       Training program for
circles

       Methods and measures to
evaluate circles

       The role that manage-
ment plays

       Other

   3.22 Actions taken by
management

       Serve on steering
committee

       Authorize meeting times
and reduction in work
hours

       Provide resource support

       Assign facilitators

       Provide continuing
support

   3.23 Actions taken by middle
management

       Meet with circle leaders
and attend some circle
meetings

       Coordinate interdepart-
mental actions

       Implement circle
recommendations

	Start	*Complete*	*Assigned to*
Develop ways to recognize circle contributions			
Maintain participative management style			
3.24 Presentation to workers	____	____	____
Answer these questions:			
What is a circle?			
Why have them?			
How is the program operated?			
Who can join?			
Why you should join?			
What training is involved?			
What are circle techniques?			
What's in it for you?			

4. Organization

4.1 GET TOP-LEVEL ACCEPTANCE AND INVOLVEMENT

4.11 Set goals and objectives	____	____	____
4.12 Get acceptance	____	____	____
4.13 Establish duties of top	____	____	____
management			
Supportive			
Participative			

4.2 DEVELOP PROGRAM STRUCTURE AND ORGANIZATION

4.21 Establish composition	____	____	____
and duties of:			
Steering committee			
Coordinator			
Facilitator			
Leaders			
Circle members			

	Start	*Complete*	*Assigned to*
4.22 Identify personnel	___	___	___
4.23 Establish meeting and agenda	___	___	___
4.24 Identify funding, budget and resource allocation	___	___	___

4.3 ESTABLISH POLICIES, PROCEDURES, AND RE-
PORTS

___   ___   ___

5. Measurement

5.1 CHECK EXISTING PRODUCTIVITY MEASURES

5.11 Overall measures	___	___	___
Total factor			
Partial factor			
5.12 Key functions and departments	___	___	___
5.13 Industry	___	___	___
5.14 Individual and team	___	___	___
5.15 White collar and indirect	___	___	___
5.16 Do measures reflect the ratio:	___	___	___

$$\frac{\text{Output}}{\text{Input}}$$

5.2 DO YOU WANT TO MEASURE QUALITY CIRCLES?

5.21 Review what others are doing	___	___	___
5.22 Get opinions within the company	___	___	___
5.23 Review objectives and relate to measurement system	___	___	___

5.3 REVIEW REASONS FOR MEASUREMENT

___   ___   ___

Direct circle activity in productive way
Sell management on support

	Start	Complete	Assigned to

"Keep score" for QC members
Choose between alternative
  problems
Gain acceptance of
  recommendations
For incentives or rewards

5.4 DETERMINE MEASUREMENT SYSTEM ⸻ ⸻ ⸻

Functional and/or depart-
  mental
Individual circle measure
Partial factor
Total factor
Industry
White collar
Other

6. Awareness

6.1 DEVELOP THE MESSAGE OF QUALITY CIRCLES AND
PRODUCTIVITY

  6.11 The *philosophy* is to open ⸻ ⸻ ⸻
    the door to communica-
    tions, innovative ideas,
    participation, and prob-
    lem solving

  6.12 Why productivity? ⸻ ⸻ ⸻
    National
    Company
    Individual
      "What's In It For Me?"

  6.13 Objectives of company ⸻ ⸻ ⸻
    program

6.2 TAKE RELATED ORGANIZATIONAL ACTIONS TO
GET AWARENESS

  6.21 Establish labor- ⸻ ⸻ ⸻
    management committee

	Start	*Complete*	*Assigned to*
and get endorsement and commitment from the union			
6.22 Get level-to-level commitment from top management to circle members	___	___	___
6.3 COMMUNICATIONS MEDIA			
6.31 Brochures and newsletters	___	___	___
6.32 External media	___	___	___
6.33 Video tapes	___	___	___
6.34 Personal letter from top operating officer	___	___	___
6.4 SPECIAL PROGRAMS			
6.41 QC incentive	___	___	___
6.42 Recognition	___	___	___
6.43 Training	___	___	___
6.44 Suggestion System	___	___	___

7. Pilot Circle Project

	Start	*Complete*	*Assigned to*
7.1 ESTABLISH CRITERIA FOR THE PILOT DEPARTMENT			
7.11 Definable and quantitative measures of quality and productivity	___	___	___
7.12 High potential (HYPO) for improvement	___	___	___
7.13 Desire to improve	___	___	___
7.14 Homogeneous work and/ or output so that pilot results can be applied in other departments	___	___	___
7.2 SEEK OUT SPONSOR			
7.21 Get top management support	___	___	___

	Start	Complete	Assigned to
7.22 Get support of a manager with the authority and the desire to implement circles in a specific area	____	____	____

7.3 DEMONSTRATE BENEFITS OF PILOT PROJECT

	Start	Complete	Assigned to
7.31 Measure improvements with measures established in 7.11	____	____	____
7.32 Establish control group for comparison	____	____	____
7.33 Communicate and publicize results	____	____	____

7.4 EXPAND CIRCLE EFFORT

	Start	Complete	Assigned to
7.41 Use pilot project to set the conditions (organization, policies, etc.) for expansion	____	____	____
7.42 Use pilot project to train facilitator and leaders	____	____	____
7.43 Expand the number of circles	____	____	____

8. Training

8.1 GET ORGANIZED

	Start	Complete	Assigned to
8.11 Research what others are doing	____	____	____
8.12 Establish duties of coordinator, facilitator, leaders	____	____	____
8.13 Determine in-house resources and capabilities	____	____	____
8.14 Inventory human resources—skills on hand and skills required; forecast training needs	____	____	____

	Start	*Complete*	*Assigned to*
8.2 TRAIN THE TRAINERS			
8.21 Select training resource	___	___	___
Visit other companies			
Select and use con-			
sultant			
Training department			
Develop own resources			
8.3 STRUCTURE THE PROGRAM			
8.31 Training methods and	___	___	___
learning materials (text,			
cases, exercises, visuals,			
etc.)			
8.32 Structure the program	___	___	___
Awareness and			
introduction			
Survey of quality circles			
Circle technical training			
Problem solving,			
pareto charts,			
data analysis, etc.			
(see chapter 9)			
8.4 IMPLEMENT, FOLLOW UP, AND DETERMINE EF-			
FECTIVENESS	___	___	___

Discussion of Selected Milestones

ACCEPTANCE

From research and our own experience the conclusion emerges that two to three years may be required
for a particular company to convert from classical-
authoritarian to participative-modern management
practice. The implications of this conclusion, as they
apply to quality circles, are simply this: *Management
must be committed to a change effort, and all persons involved in the change must be involved in its initiation.*

The basic problem in this change effort is that the participatory chain is only as strong as its weakest link. If any link breaks, the process of participative management, and hence quality circles, comes to a halt. Management, from first-line supervisor to top executive, must emphasize that communal problem solving is an integral part of everyone's job.

To *"sell"* or get acceptance from management, we are concerned with three levels: (1) top management, (2) middle management, and (3) supervisory or first-line management. In all of these we want to avoid the "fast fix" syndrome. In other words, quality circles are not another short-term "management" program that attempts to apply a Band-Aid to problems of human relations, cost reduction, or productivity. Upfront acceptance will avoid making a manager think that his or her role is just to transmit a directive from the top, stating that the company is going to have quality circles.

In general, it is easier to convince top executives than it is to get acceptance from the other two levels. Says Rosabeth Moss Kanter, a sociologist and a consultant in the field: "I find it's easy to get top executives on board. They like to be intellectual, they're impressed by professors, they're intrigued by concepts, they tend to be moved by examples of how other companies are doing it."

Middle-level managers are more reluctant to endorse quality circles, particularly if it means worker or subordinate participation. Many of them have spent their working lives polishing the technical skills required for survival in the classical hierarchical organization. Acceptance of quality circles requires a new human resource skill involving collaboration with people who work for them.

Front-line supervisors are also reluctant to endorse quality circles if they are asked to perform as leaders or if they perceive that they are being coerced into the program. Acceptance at this level is largely a function of how well they are "sold" on the value of circles to themselves, the workers, and the company, as well as the priorities attached to circles by their supervisors and other line management.

MEASUREMENT

Two questions arise when considering the measurement of quality circles. First is the question of "if" — should they be measured at all? The answer to this question is largely a function of your objectives. The "how" of measurement is easier to answer. If you have a productivity program planned or in place, the measurement of quality circles can become a subset of that program.

AWARENESS

If quality circles are to gain acceptance and subsequently to work, we need an approach to bring *awareness* to both management and workers about the importance of productivity and the role of quality circles in achieving productivity. *Awareness* is the necessary step in achieving *participation* and *commitment*. Employees want to know what's going on in their company, and they cannot very well help the improvement program if they do not know nor understand what's going on.

Awareness is simply a matter of communications: originating the appropriate message in terms the recipient can understand; getting organized; and choosing the correct media and programs to complete the process. Common sense and the experience of others indicate that an awareness program can be designed by selecting the appropriate action from these:

- The message of productivity
- Getting organized
- Communication media: meetings
- Communication media: printed

- Programs
- Training

The Message of Productivity. Gaining acceptance of productivity improvement is largely a matter of understanding its importance to the national economy, to the viability of the company, and to the future job security and life-style of the individual. Most people will accept the need for productivity if the argument, "sales pitch," or message is phrased in terms that demonstrate how their needs may be met. Some reasons to answer the question "Why productivity?" are the following:

National

- Maintain the American economic system at a level that improves or even sustains our current standard of living.
- Ensure the survival of the private enterprise system.
- Provide a lasting solution to the problems of inflation and unemployment.

Company

- Strengthen our competitive position in domestic and world markets.
- Generate funds for capital investment and expansion.
- Meet the pressures of rising costs.
- Enhance customer satisfaction.
- Improve our competitive edge.

- Make higher return on investment.
- Provide more job and advancement opportunities.

Individual

- Reduce waste and conserve resources.
- Maintain job security.
- Increase leisure time.
- Improve job satisfaction and working conditions.
- Improve communications by means of worker involvement.
- Maintain wages at fair levels in real terms.

General Motors considers quality circles to be part of a larger effort called Quality of Work Life. Indeed, circles are the essential component of that effort. In the following, a joint union-management document answers the question, What's in it for me?

How Will QWL Circles Help Me?

QWL circles are designed to help everyone. It is a program designed to improve communications between management and the employee in order to solve the many problems that confront all of us who do similar work. The problems are not always product quality problems. They could be health and safety problems, environmental problems, or any problem that contributes to inferior working conditions that lead to an inferior product. The "bottom line" is to build the best GM products possible. Everyone gains. Everyone's job becomes easier because we are working together, thinking together, and solving problems together. We are then communicating better by participating in QWL circles.

Communications Media

Meetings

In addition to the meetings conducted by groups specifically organized for the purpose of productivity improvement (e.g., Productivity Council, Steering Committee, PITS, QCs), the topic can be included on the agenda of a wide variety of other regular company meetings. Conferences, discussion programs, round tables, and association meetings provide a sample of opportunities to raise the topic.

Don't overlook *customers and suppliers.* These two groups are part of the effort and can lend valuable assistance when they are part of the "team."

Special Media Vehicles

Most companies have a number of standard vehicles for communicating to a variety of audiences. These range from annual reports to bulletin boards and generally are not adequate to bring awareness to a program as important as productivity improvement. Although these standard communications channels can and should be used to promote the idea, consideration should be given to designing *special* media vehicles for this special purpose. Consider these:

- Employee *attitudinal surveys* to determine receptivity to and misunderstandings about productivity. Such surveys can also serve the additional purposes of indicating training needs, promoting involvement, and serving the purpose for follow-up action.
- *Brochures and newsletters* help to keep interest alive and bring understanding and awareness.

These media can include such items as publicity and photographs of team or quality circle improvement efforts and achievements, rewards and recognition, industry news, and a variety of information articles, cases, and techniques.

- *External media* such as local newspapers, trade journals, and association magazines give publicity to the company and its people and promote a feeling of pride in achievement.

- *Videotapes* are being produced by some companies. These tapes can serve the dual purpose of providing awareness and training. The content can range from informative to substantive; uses can range from introductory to basic training in skills related to teams and individuals.

- The *personal letter* from the top operating officer to the employees at their homes can be effective. It can give the reasons for the effort ("Why productivity?") and include a rundown of company actions. The letter can help to allay the fears of the employees concerning job security. It might also include a few words from the union president, reiterating a stand for collective bargaining and productivity and explaining the role of quality circles.

- In addition to the awareness effort itself, supplementary and/or related *programs* can serve the additional purpose of promoting awareness. A good title for such an approach could be "The Productivity Incentive Program." It could be both for individuals and teams or circles. This effort is broader in scope than the traditional "cost-reduction" program and incentives could include such actions as:

    Recognition of each incentive submission with gift certificate
    Monthly or quarterly luncheons with plant management for functional winners
    Publication of winners by function in newsletter or digest

Publicity photographs of winners posted on announcement boards

- *Training* is perhaps the best way to bring awareness of productivity and quality circles.

- Another way to publicize circles is to tie the program in with your existing suggestion system. This system and circles are complementary provided you have been having some reasonable success with and acceptance of the suggestion system.

PILOT CIRCLE PROJECT

Some managers are justifiably reluctant to undertake the installation of quality circles on a company-wide basis. They prefer to "test the water" with a pilot project. There are two advantages to this approach. First, it allows you to select those areas and those personnel that have a higher potential for success. It follows that, if you achieve success in the pilot project, you have a greater probability of acceptance and success in subsequent circles.

A second advantage of trying a pilot project first is that you avoid the possibility of embarrassment and expense of failure throughout the company. Moreover, this larger failure, should it occur, may preclude another try at a later time. The smaller failure of a pilot project, on the other hand, does not stop you from undertaking a second project in another location or at a later date.

Quality of Work Life Programs

This book has addressed itself to the topic of *quality circles*. However, the reader should be aware that *quality of work life* (QWL) programs (of which quality circles are an essential part) are growing in American industry. A brief description of QWL is provided at this point in the event that the reader wishes to consider explanding QCs in his or her firm to a broader program involving both productivity and/or QWL.

Quality of Working Life is a term made popular by Richard Nixon. It is an accelerating movement in the United States and in Europe as well. It is being promoted by employees, by some unions, by government, and by many management groups and companies. Those individuals who take the time to understand the principles of QWL recognize that the concept goes hand in glove with productivity improvement and quality circles. Each reinforces the other. In the words of Theodore Mills, director of the American Quality of Work Center, "I don't know of a single instance in which improved quality of working life didn't lead to improved productivity."

*"Spacetronics" [a pseudonym] is the primary supplier of airborne computers required for the guidance system of Minuteman ICBMs. Quality is essential and quality assurance a major concern. In an effort to improve quality and productivity, the firm established a QWL program that included the elements of participative management and problem solving and group or team goal setting accompanied by feedback and training. Three thousand people were eventually involved, and the results included a 20% to 30% increase in productivity with a 30% to 50% improvement in quality.**

WHAT IS QWL?

To help you understand QWL, we will summarize what it *is* and what it *is not*. What QWL *is not* is the concern with the environment and corporate social responsibility reflected in the movement of Ralph Nader. What it *is not* is the philosophical movement in which a

---

* Adapted from John R. Hinrichs, *Practical Management for Productivity* (New York: Van Nostrand Reinhold Company, 1978).

greater understanding of self and of relations to others, and a closer relationship with nature are stressed. What QWL *is* is the approach to a working environment that increases output by better human-resource management while at the same time achieving a *more satisfying and rewarding life at work.*

One of General Motors' most successful QWL efforts has been at the Tarrytown (New York) assembly plant where the company's worst facility turned around and won GM's highest quality award as the firm's top unit. The United Auto Workers local president said, "The grievance load has been cut from 2,000 to 20 and everybody is more of an integral part of the structure than ever before. What the [QWL] program has done is create an atmosphere at the workplace that is no different than it is at home. You're not turned off when you walk in the factory gate."

The actions that need to be taken to provide a satisfying and rewarding life at work are fortunately the same actions that are required for human-resource motivation and hence productivity. We repeat that this is fortunate because it simplifies both the QWL and the productivity problems. We have already commented on the connection between them.

COMPONENTS OF A QWL PROGRAM

The major components of a QWL program can be summarized as follows:

- *Participation and Participative Management.* This involves the sloughing off of the old-fashioned idea that management is omnipotent and that labor can be manipulated. It involves a recognition that employees can be responsible, mature, and knowledgeable about work affecting them, that they want to be involved. It is possible to implement managerial approaches and programs that build employee involvement and *common goals*. Employees have both the potential and the desire to contribute to problem solving and innovation for improvement.

- *Team Organization.* QWL problem-solving groups, which are referred to as "quality circles" or "productivity improvement teams" (PITS), are a recent organizational innovation designed to break through the structure of the functional departments or to improve the operation of an ongoing but specific task or problem. Aside from contributing to the adaptability of the team and its receptivity to new ideas, membership in such groups can heighten motivation and commitment to effective performance.

- *Job Development.* This component of QWL ensures that individuals use their talent, ability, and knowledge. This means that employees are allowed to have the maximum amount of autonomy concerning how a job is to be done. A person's commitment to a job is a function of the amount of control he or she has over it. Job-design concepts also take account of the skills and knowledge of the team or group in order to take advantage of the diverse abilities and the synergy of the group.

- *Incentives and Feedback.* Continuing motivation and productivity depend upon the formulation of realistic objectives or targets and the existence of feedback concerning progress. The "loop" is therefore a process of goal setting, feedback, and reinforcement.

Avoiding the Pitfalls

Lest we be accused of utopianism in describing quality circles in this book, we must remind you that this road to quality and productivity contains a few pitfalls. Nowhere have we stated that the installation of quality circles is a snap, and nowhere have we indicated it would be without problems. So, as a matter of "caveat," or "don't say we didn't tell you," it would be wise to look at some areas of potential difficulty.

OBJECTIONS TO QUALITY CIRCLES

1. *Union objections.* Unions may perceive quality circles as another attempt by management to squeeze more productivity from the workers without sharing the rewards, or as a system that will bring management and workers closer together— thus reducing the need for the union. The unions may fear that increased productivity by circles will result in layoffs. In earlier chapters we emphasized the need to reach an early understanding with the union.

2. *Takes time from the job.* A management that thinks increased efficiency can only come from better technology or management guidance will object to the time circles take from the job, as well as the possibility of overtime pay.

3. *Hostility of middle managers and supervisors.* We have discussed previously the fear of this group that the quality circle program challenges its power and authority. The circle concept represents a change from the "old way of doing things."

4. *Lack of credibility on the part of workers, due to past management practices.* They may perceive circles as a means of management manipulation, or as "just another program" being forced on them.

5. *Past experience with a suggestion program.* Workers and middle management may have experienced negative results from suggestion programs which did not work, or were not acted upon.

They may feel that quality circles are simply another effort in this direction.

6. *Quality circles mean change.* This can mean a supervisor's resistance to the change of management style or his or her span of control. Members may resist a change in the workplace. In some instances, they may resist having to accept more responsibility for the quality of work.

ROADBLOCKS TO QUALITY CIRCLES

One of the major roadblocks to the long-term effectiveness of quality circles is the use of short-term factors to measure worker and management effectiveness. Robert Ostlund, a Honeywell engineer assigned to evaluate the company's circle effectiveness, stated, "Short-term benefits are 'nice' and a 'bonus' but are not to be confused with long-term goals. Teams are a long-term commitment to a change in management style, not a short-term program. We are certainly encouraged by the short-term productivity gains because solving productivity problems is one of the goals. But improving employee attitudes and developing employee skills and potential are equally important. It will take time to be sure of these long-term outcome measures."

1. *Inadequate training.* An inadequately trained circle leader unable to give a sense of direction and leadership to the group can negatively affect the circle's ability to perform constructively. A lack of leader and member training in the tools and techniques of problem solving defeats the purpose of the group in problem solving and action planning.

2. *Poor management response to the circle.* This includes management support of the group as it develops into a working entity, as well as timely response to circle suggestions. Management's fail-

ure to act on circle recommendations in a timely manner or impatience with results can have a frustrating effect on circle morale.

3. *Unrealistic expectations.* This can include too much push, too soon, for financial review or increase in productivity. A quality circle is not an "overnight" miracle of results, particularly in the beginning of the program. An overemphasis on quick financial return or productivity increase may force the circle into a hurried proposal lacking in statistical data and sound planning.

4. *Vague measures.* Lack of skills in measures, problem definition and analysis, and problem solution may result in a project or proposal that is vague and disorganized.

Other roadblocks which hamper the "nitty-gritty" work process of circles include setting unobtainable goals, selecting problems which are too difficult for the circle, scheduling problems, and using too much or too little publicity.

Dr. David Amsden and Dr. Robert T. Amsden, in their article, *"QC Circles: A Challenge to ASQC,"* indulged in a bit of prophecy when they stated: "Attacks will come: some managers who are over-eager; some organizational experts will try to organize it into a grave of red-tape; faddists will attempt to bring in transcendental meditation; some academicians will attempt to over-research it and make it too theoretical; indeed, some will overemphasize the statistical tools; and other attacks will come." Quality circles will work—just avoid the pitfalls!

9

Quality Circle Training Techniques

QC Circle members —Let's study.

Slogan adopted by DR. KAORU ISHIKAWA,
founder of Japanese quality circles

A major factor in the Japanese productivity and quality revolution has been the extensive training in quality at all levels from top management to production worker. Indeed, continuous learning is a way of life in Japanese industry.

We have outlined elsewhere in this book how productivity and quality are two sides of the same coin. Yet traditionally the American worker has not been trained in either dimension. Training in problem identification and prevention can help overcome this shortcoming.

Professor W. Edwards Deming, the man who started the Japanese productivity and quality revolution, concluded: "Folklore has it in America that a plant manager can not excel in both quality and production. Ask any plant manager. He will tell you that it is either or. If he insists on quality, he will fall behind in production: that if he pushes production, quality will suffer. This folklore is held by people that know not what quality is, nor how to improve it." Deming further stated that quality is achieved by improving the *process* and that improved quality equals improved productivity. These improvements in turn will result in lower cost, as well as greater satisfaction for both employees and customers.

Because the major focus in quality circle training is on problem identification and solution, we will focus on these techniques. The recipients of training are (1) the circle leader, and (2) circle members.

Leader Training

The effectiveness of a circle is largely a function of leader performance because it is that individual who conducts circle meetings and in some cases the training of circle members as well. *In addition to training in the same techniques given to circle members*, the leader is given exposure to the personal skills necessary for effectiveness in leading a group. These concepts and skills may include:

- *Group dynamics.* The interaction of people in group situations. How to achieve consensus and resolve conflict.
- *Motivation.* Concepts and principles of human motivation. How to use quality circles to meet members' needs. Job satisfaction and its relation to circle participation.
- *Communications.* Why communications is perhaps the number one objective of circles. The importance of communication for group functioning. Perception, feedback, barriers to communication, and other traditional principles.
- *Leadership.* How personal leadership style can impact on group effectiveness. Identification and development of leadership style.

Training for Quality Circle Members

The general purpose or output expected from member training is the identification, solution, and presentation of problems having to do with productivity and quality. The process is summarized in this concept:

			Recommendation
Problem →	Problem →	Problem →	to
Identification	Selection	Analysis	Management

A typical training program in problem-solving tools and techniques usually consists of the following modules:

- *Introduction to Quality Circles*
- *Brainstorming*
- *Data Collection and Display*
- *Problem Analysis*

    Cause-and-effect Diagram (Fishbone)
    Pareto Analysis
- *Presentation to Management*

INTRODUCTION TO QUALITY CIRCLES

The purpose of this introductory module is to introduce the concepts and the techniques that circle members will use in subsequent meetings and to provide an overview of what constitutes a successful program. Among the topics covered are:

- The background and development of the QC movement
- Objectives of the program
- The concept of personal and team development
- The policy of voluntary participation
- Circle projects are group efforts
- Circles have the support of management
- Innovation is encouraged
- Rules for circle meetings

BRAINSTORMING

In quality circle activities, the sine qua non is full participation. If reliance is placed on the opinions and the ideas of a select few, the "team participation" concept is defeated, and the circle may come to an early demise. Brainstorming is one effective method in helping to unlock the group's creative power. It can be defined as a *group of people using their collective imaginative powers to create ideas and solutions.*

The brainstorming technique is useful in the four major steps involved in a circle's operation (e.g., problem identification, problem selection, problem analysis and management presentation). General guidelines for brainstorming include the following:

1. Select a problem within the group's work area. Select the problem in precise terms.
2. Solicit ideas from each member in rotation until new ideas have been exhausted.
3. Strive for quantity of ideas without judging quality.
4. Accumulate ideas for visual presentation so that the group can then rank them for decision making.

"Do's and don't's" should consist of the following:

Do	Don't
Encourage total participation	Criticize ideas
Encourage quantity	Judge ideas during brain-
Encourage freewheeling	storming
Establish clearly defined goals	Tune out or turn individual
Encourage an open attitude toward suggestions	members off

The advantage of brainstorming is that it is applicable in determining causes when using the cause-and-effect diagram, in Pareto analysis, and in other problem areas of decision making. In addition, brainstorming continues the training in the participative teamwork necessary to develop expertise in problem solving.

DATA COLLECTION AND DISPLAY

Because much, if not most, of circle time is spent on (1) problem analysis, and (2) problem prevention, the collection of information is an essential part of both training and operations. Three elementary techniques for *data collection*, usually part of the training program, are: *sampling, check sheets,* and *data display.*

Sampling is frequently useful in the process of data collection leading to problem analysis. After all, it is prohibitively expensive in time and money to collect data on 100% of the population of the problem or the process under consideration. The sampling process includes these steps: (1) identify the "population" (universe), (2) determine the size of the sample from a sampling table, (3) select the sample, (4) gather the data, (5) display the data, (6) make a conclusion or prediction or analyze the problem based upon the data.

Check sheets are an aid in assembling and compiling data surrounding a problem. A check sheet is used to collect data on a process to determine if any unusual or unwanted elements are present. Dr. Ishikawa defined the functions of a check sheet as:

- Production process distribution checks
- Defective item checks
- Defect location checks
- Defect cause checks
- Checkup confirmation checks

To illustrate the use of check sheets, let's examine the case of the National Machine Tool Company, manufacturer of chuck jaws for the metals industry. A chuck jaw is a holding device used on a machine for metal turning and indexing.

Quality circle members identified (through brain-storming) the number one problem as "loss of time due to reworked jobs." The circle agreed that in order to determine the cause of excessive reworked jobs, it would be necessary to find out which department or departments were experiencing excessive rework. As a result, data were collected and recorded on the check sheet shown in figure 9-1. It is evident from this check sheet that department number 55 has excessive re-work.

Weeks

Department		No. 1	No. 2	No. 3	No. 4	No. 5	No. 6	No. 7	No. 8	TOTAL
	11		/		//		/			4
	66	/		/		//		//	/	7
	55	///	/	//	//	/	7//L	//	////	20
	22	/	//		///	//		/	/	10
	Other			/		/		//		4

FIGURE 9-1. Check Sheet of Reworked Jobs.

DATA DISPLAY

After data are collected, they can be converted into a variety of forms for *display and analysis*. The most common of these are shown in figure 9-2.

- A *control chart* reflects an on-going control of a process and signals an alarm when the process exceeds the control limits. When the line moves beyond the control limit [dotted line in figure 9-2(a)], it can signal a problem.

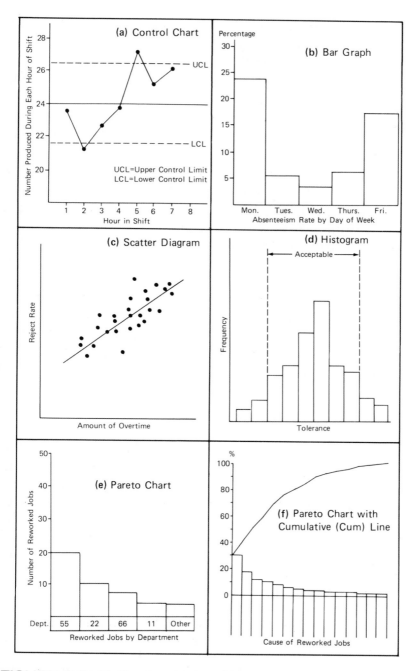

FIGURE 9-2. Methods of Displaying Data.

- A *bar graph* or column graph summarizes and presents data in an easily understood manner.

- A *scatter diagram* depicts the relationship between two kinds of data, and the relationship forms a pattern.

- A *histogram* is a vertical bar graph showing the distribution of data in terms of the frequency of occurrence for specific values of data.

- A *pareto diagram* is the most widely used statistical tool in problem analysis. Indeed, it is almost universal in quality circle deliberations. It is a graphic way of summarizing data in order to focus attention on the main reason(s) why some result is occurring and to lead to a cause-and-effect relationship.

- The *cumulative distribution line*, or "cum" line, is an additional dimension to the pareto diagram. The "cum" line displays the cumulative distribution of events by percentage. The total of all events is 100%.

PROBLEM ANALYSIS

Cause-and-effect Diagram. The cause-and-effect diagram, known as the C&E diagram or sometimes as the "fishbone" diagram, was developed and named by Professor Kaoru Ishikawa of the University of Tokyo in 1950. This process is not limited to quality circles as it can be used in a variety of circumstances. It is an excellent tool for organizing and documenting potential causes of problems in all areas and at all levels in the organization. In other words, it is appropriate for white-collar and administrative areas, as well as for production applications. In addition, the approach can be used for top management as well as shop floor problems.

Returning to the case of the National Machine Tool Company (page 181), the fishbone *diagram was used to brain-*

storm possible causes of "excessive reworked jobs." The result of that brainstorming session is shown in figure 9-3 which also illustrates the construction and use of the C&E (fishbone) diagram.

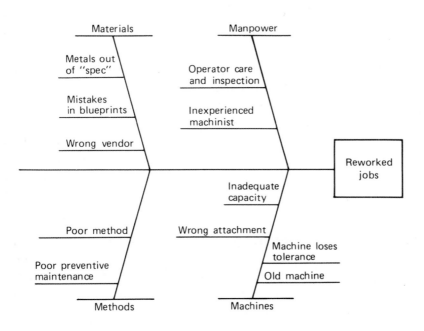

FIGURE 9-3. Cause-and-effect diagram.

Briefly stated, the C&E technique as demonstrated in the National Machine Tool case above consists of defining an *effect* (reworked jobs) and then determining its contributing factors (*causes*).

Cause-and-effect diagrams are drawn to clearly illustrate the various causes affecting product quality and productivity by sorting out and relating the causes. In the brainstorming session the causes given by the circle can be listed on the blackboard or flip charts and later transferred to the cause-and-effect diagram. A more experienced group might prepare the diagram directly from the causes given. Some reasons for using the cause-and-effect diagram are the following:

1. The diagram is a guide for discussion. It serves as a focus on the subject at hand and discourages straying from the topic. The diagram serves as a measure of progress and how far the discussion has progressed.
2. The diagram is an educational tool. It encourages full participation from the group and encourages shared knowledge regarding the subject at hand.
3. The diagram encourages data-gathering. In listing the causes for a diagram, many instances occur where the cause needs to be supported with additional data to test its validity; this "zeros" in on the need for more information in attacking the problem.

As can be seen from figure 9-3, a cause-and-effect diagram is rather straightforward in its use. The EFFECT is blocked off at the right end of a horizontal line. The diagonal lines lead to four subheadings, usually materials, manpower, methods, and machines—the four Ms. Other headings can be used depending upon the particular problem at hand. The sub-subheadings are the causes elicited from the group during the brainstorming session.

A general guide to constructing cause-and-effect diagrams will include the following steps:

1. Identify the *effect* for which causes are to be determined in clear concise terms.
2. Establish *goals* for the brainstorming activities as to measurements of improvement, and within a certain time span.
3. Construct the diagram upon which the causes are to be listed in such a way that it is visible to the entire group.

4. Use the "rules" of brainstorming to record all suggestions for the causes.

5. "Incubate" the diagram, i.e., keep it on display for a time to encourage further suggestions.

6. Diagnose the project.

Pareto Analysis. Dr. J. M. Juran popularized the term, "the pareto principle" while teaching quality control methods to the Japanese following World War II. This process is derived from *pareto's law* named after the Italian economist, Alfredo Pareto (1848-1923). Pareto's law presents the concept that any cause that results from a multiplicity of effects is primarily a result of the impact from a minor percentage of all the causes. Conversely, a majority of the causative factors play a minor role in the observed effect. In his study of the distribution of wealth and income during his day, Pareto observed that wealth was concentrated in the hands of a few while the great majority of the population was in poverty.

This technique is similar to the "80-20" rule whose concept is explained as follows:

1. 80% of inventory value is in 20% of your inventory items.

2. 80% of sales volume comes from 20% of the customers.

3. 80% of overdue accounts are owed by 20% of the customers.

Some examples where pareto analysis is a universal tool include:

1. A problem in inventory reduction where there are large numbers of separate items.

2. An analysis of sales volume by product.

3. A breakdown of accounts receivable by dollar amount and customer.

This type of analysis is sometimes called the separa-
tion of the *vital few* from the *trivial many*. Thus, from the
above examples, we can see that the pareto principle is a
universal tool for sorting any *conglomerate mixture* into
two neat piles, the vital few and the trivial many. This
tool is a fundamental one in the operation of quality circles for identifying the important problems and establishing priorities. Dr. Juran, in his book, *Managerial
Breakthrough*, stated it succinctly: "The vital few are
everywhere, but masquerading under a variety of
aliases. In their more benevolent forms they are known
by such names as key accounts or star salesmen. In their
weak moments they are known as the bottlenecks,
chronic drinkers, deadbeats, most wanted criminals, critical components."

*In the case of the National Machine Tool Company, pre-
viously described, the data from the* check sheet *(figure
9-1) was transcribed and converted to the* pareto chart
*shown in figure 9-4. It becomes evident from an examina-
tion of the chart that the major problem can be traced to
department 55.*

A more sophisticated problem of sorting a conglomerate mixture into the vital few and the trival many is
illustrated by a cause-and-effect diagram (figure 9-5) and
a subsequent pareto analysis (figure 9-6) for a specific
case. This case involves a company using plastics for
printing and packaging materials. The company was concerned over the amount of defects coming off the machine
production line, such as misprints, print out of register,
warpage, etc.

The circle selected this as a project and through
brainstorming prepared a cause-and-effect diagram as in
figure 9-5. After a thorough study of the causes and the
effect, the circle agreed that a monitor would be ap-
pointed to check the causes of all defects over a four-week
period. From the information collected over this period,

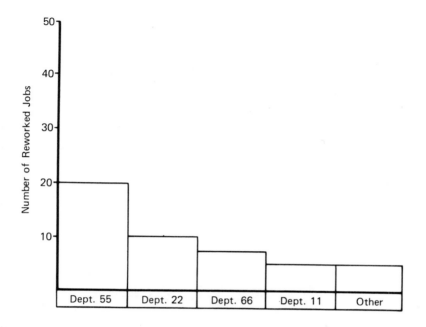

FIGURE 9-4. Pareto chart of reworked jobs.

through the use of a check sheet, a pareto chart was developed for the circle meeting (figure 9-6).

As can be seen from the pareto chart in figure 9-6, the vital few, e.g., "tension on material" and "tracking," make up 46% of the causes for defects. This graphically illustrates the major areas that need attention.

The pareto chart also points out a simple, though often overlooked, fact in setting a goal to reduce defects by a certain percentage, i.e., reducing the 28% "tension on material" by 50% results in a 14% reduction, whereas reducing the 2% "register slippage" by 50% only results in a 1% reduction. Yet it may have taken the same amount of time and effort to reduce both causes.

The curved line in figure 9-6 illustrates the cumulative distribution of defects by percentage; however, there

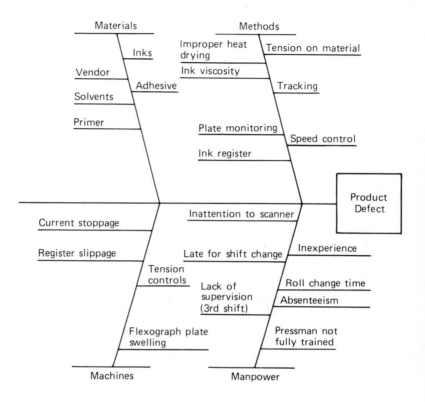

FIGURE 9-5. Cause-and-effect diagram.

is another use of the pareto graph which incorporates dollar amounts. The circle could have determined the total costs of the machine defects over the same four-week period by working with the engineering department, accounts, and possibly personnel, to determine costs in materials, overhead and labor. As an example, if the total costs of the machine defects over a four-week period amounted to $3,000.00, this amount would represent the vertical line of the pareto chart. The item, "tension on material," representing 28%, would amount to $840.00 on the vertical line. If the group is to obtain its

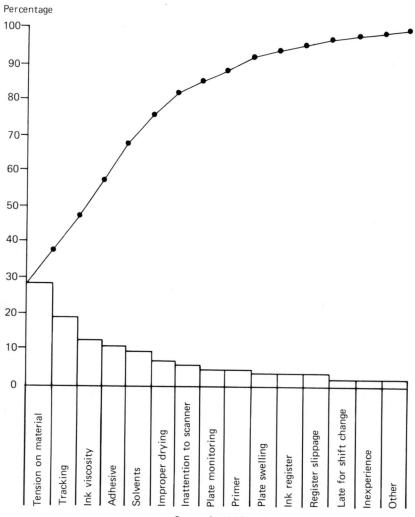

FIGURE 9-6. Pareto chart with cumulative total.

goal of reducing defects by 50%, the resultant pareto chart would then show a total in dollars of $1,500.00, with a different configuration of items listed.

PRESENTATION TO MANAGEMENT

We have discussed in an earlier chapter the value of esprit de corps which can exist within a quality circle when its members are working toward a common goal. Preparing for a presentation to management may generate such a spirit of team participation and the desire to complete a successful project. Generally, there are two types of presentations: (1) when the circle has planned a project which will require extra manpower, costs, or equipment and needs the approval of management for the project, and (2) when the circle has completed a project and presents the results to management. In most instances, the supervisor or middle management, or possibly a member of the steering committee, will be aware of a planned project which will not need a presentation to management for approval. In this instance, the circle will make a presentation to management at the project's completion.

The presentation is a team approach. The entire circle meets face-to-face with management, with a chosen member of the circle making the presentation. The presentation is a team effort; everyone has participated in the analysis of the project, and everyone is a part of the presentation.

It is here that the visual impact of quality circle tools and techniques creates an impressive example of team participation. The circle member will present the problem the group selected and through the use of charts, posters, or overhead projector, follow through the process of brainstorming, cause-and-effect diagram, data collecting, the pareto chart, etc. In this manner the logical process of problem solving is explained and illustrated.

Circle achievements are shown in quality control improvements, cost savings, or productivity improvements. Through this presentation, the circle is given management approval and recognition. Through this approval, management has been given a motivational tool for the workers while the workers have received the motivator "recognition."

SOME CONCLUDING WORDS ON THE SUBJECT OF QUALITY CIRCLES

Throughout this book we have emphasized that the success of quality circles depends upon a certain management perspective. Experience has also proven the truth of this idea. The classical "authoritarian management style" is no longer conducive to productivity improvement in the workplace. The changing worker attitudes of today, the younger age group entering the labor market, and the desire for a "piece of the action" demands a change in the interaction between labor and management.

The quality circle process, in order to be successful, requires a "participative management" atmosphere where workers feel that they are a part of the team and a part of the results in the industry's endeavor.

The chief executive who, with a "now hear this" approach, orders that quality circles be installed and that a short-term report on results be given handicaps the endeavor from the beginning. Pity the consultant or the company facilitator as he or she is faced with sleepless nights and frustrating days trying to get the program "off the ground."

Without preaching the gospel of the behavioral scientists, let it be said that a participative management which understands the motivational needs of workers is the key to successful quality circles.

Index